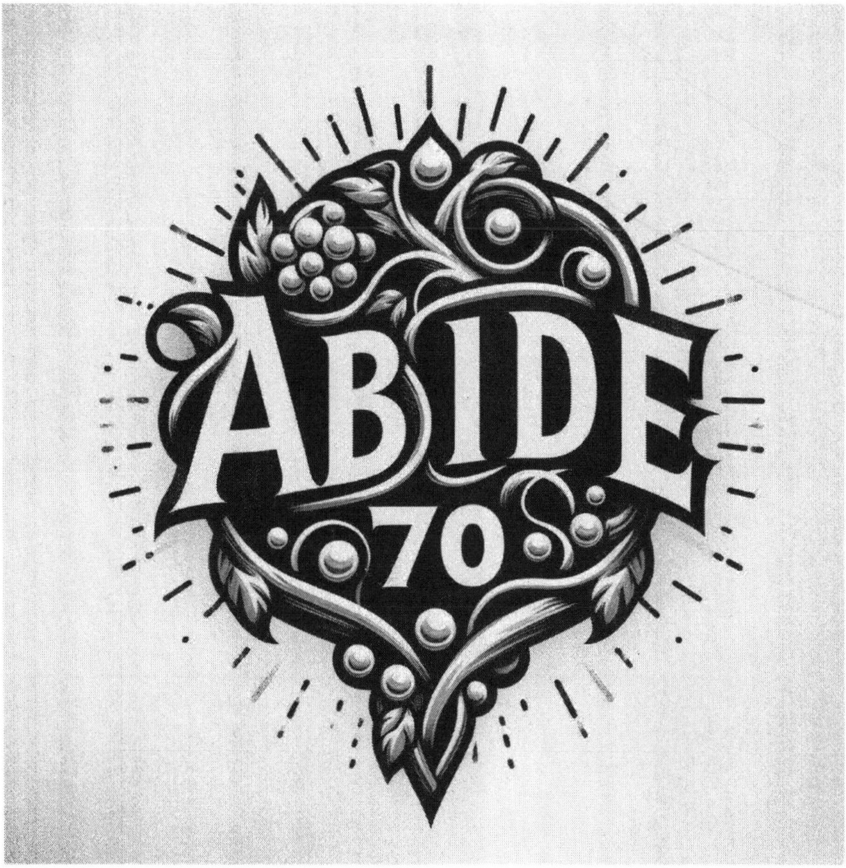

V2

Abide70:

10 Week Men's Spiritual Formation and Accountability Groups

Introduction to Abide70

A few short years ago, I was ensnared by sin, distant from God, and suffering from insomnia, anxiety, and depression. I was an absent husband and a poor leader of my family. I wanted to stop my habitual secret sin, but would keep going back to it after repeated attempts to stop.

I believed the worst possible situation was that I would be found out. The idea of confessing my sin to God, my wife and to others felt impossible—the consequences would be too great for me to bear.

But I can testify that God is merciful: The Holy Spirit and my sin could not live together inside of me, and the Lord used the testimonies of others to begin to soften my heart. Following a marriage conference, my wife asked me a single simple question:

"I know that you have been struggling—is there anything that you want to confess to me?"

My immediate response was out of the flesh, a quick and defensive—"No."

But then, all the walls came crumbling down. The Holy Spirit convicted me of my sin and the answer came— "Yes."

Confession followed, then more confession, then more. Years of hiding and running away from God and running to my sin, years of fear of being found out were over and finally, finally, I didn't have to hide anymore. After confession came

repentance. Then freedom. Then boasting in the work of Jesus Christ in my life. Make no mistake, all of this was humbling, even humiliating at times, but as I have shared my story with other men, God has used my weakness and sin to point to Christ's forgiveness and his power to release prisoners from their chains. I get the joy of helping other men run from their sin and into the open arms of Jesus. This is my purpose.

True freedom requires each of us to feel the weight and see the destruction of our own sin and take responsibility for it. It requires us to have a desire to be forgiven and made free by the blood of Jesus. He is where we must go for our initial forgiveness and salvation, and then he is where we must go daily for sustenance, for growth and sanctification. This daily pursuit of God is the basis for Abide70.

I am the vine; you are the branches. Whoever abides in me and I in him, he it is that bears much fruit, for apart from me you can do nothing. If anyone does not abide in me he is thrown away like a branch and withers; and the branches are gathered, thrown into the fire, and burned. If you abide in me, and my words abide in you, ask whatever you wish, and it will be done for you. By this my Father is glorified, that you bear much fruit and so prove to be my disciples. As the Father has loved me, so have I loved you. Abide in my love. If you keep my commandments, you will abide in my love, just as I have kept my Father's commandments and abide in his love. These things I have spoken to you, that my joy may be in you, and that your joy may be full. (John 15:5-11)

When we abide with Jesus Christ, finding our satisfaction

and our identity in him, we bear fruit. It is in the power of the Holy Spirit that we embrace our call to lay down our lives, serving others.

Abide70 groups are spiritual formation and accountability small groups of 3-7 men, meeting together for 10 weeks to:

- Abide in Christ (John 15:4).
- Earnestly seek God's face (Psalm 27:8)
- Know God (John 17:3)
- Turn from the practice of sin (Acts 3:19, 1 John 3:9); especially sexual sin (I Corinthians 6:18)
- Turn away from ourselves, love others by laying down our lives for others: (John 15:13, I John 3:16-18)
- Train in the word (2 Timothy 3:16-17)
- Disciple and lead other men to do the same. (Matthew 28:18-20)

This is what we are called to—to contend for one another. We all have a choice before us daily:

Will we worship ourselves, or will we worship Christ?

Commitment

For Abide70 to be effective, you need to be able to commit to participate in-person aiming for at least 8 out of 10 weeks. Groups need to be proximate, you need to live or work close enough to meet in person, because this is where real work is done. Assess the season of your life that you are in to determine whether the time commitment and in person meetings are a probability. There will be ample opportunity for there to be excuses to not go through this exercise, so you need to stack the deck in your favor. Maybe you aren't ready to grow, maybe you are just in an emergency mode—see the **"I Need Help Now"** section in the appendix.

For this limited amount of time—70 days— I am calling you to do something difficult, something that most people don't do—to break old habits, be uncomfortable, stop turning to the flesh for comfort, to deny yourself and follow Christ. This isn't about teeth-gritting drudgery, but a turning off the constant buzz of the world so that you can learn to hear the sweet voice of Christ that is calling to you—to do this, most men need to establish new, healthier Biblical rhythms. For 70 days the expectation is that you set new patterns:

Wake up early (Psalm 119:147): Get up an hour earlier or more than your alarm goes off today— reorder your day to orient around the spiritual disciplines, establish a calendar of rhythms so you can prioritize first things first.
Pray (Galatians 6:2, Hebrews 4:16 I Thessalonians 5:17): Write prayer requests down from the group members and following up. Pray bold prayers in the power of the Holy Spirit that lives in us.
Share (1 John 1:9): Grow in sharing our burdens, regularly confessing sin and repenting with one another.
Read (2 Timothy 3:16-17): Set a Bible reading goal here so that other men can hold you accountable. Suggestion: spend time in the word for at least 30 min, progressing to 1 hr/day or more after the first month.
Redeem time (Ephesians 5:15-16): Listen to sermons or worship music during drive time, down time, bored time.

Share with your core group what you will listen to—avoid news and negative media.

Fast from media (Psalm 101:2-4): Limit cell phone use, fast from Social Media. No Netflix. No games. (Resource: Smartphone to Dumbphone Guide, in the appendix)

Physical challenge (1 Corinthians 9:26-27): Make your own goal and be accountable to it: 30 minutes of exercise/day, cold showers, 100 pushups/day, fast 1x weekly, etc.

Accountability (1 Thessalonians 5:11): Reach out to the team of men daily, Reach out to other men who are on your heart weekly. Evangelize. Reach out to non-Christians regularly.

Memorization (Colossians 3:16) : Hide God's word in your heart where no one can take it from you.

If you don't believe in the saving power and you aren't a follower of Christ, none of this will change you—It will be action without power. I admonish you—believe in and place your dependence on Jesus as your Lord and Savior—it is in his power that you overcome sin.

If you are a believer, the next page is a chart for you to write down your goals in each of these areas. Take a picture with your phone and share your goals with the other men in your group. Give them permission to ask you about how you are doing in each of these areas. If you need more space, write it on a separate piece of paper.

Discipline	Goal	Frequency
Wake up early	0500 wake up (example)	Daily
Prayer		
Share		
Read (Bible)		
Redeem time		
Fast from media		
Physical Challenge		
Accountability		
Memorization		
Other		
Other 2		

Abide70 is 10 Weekly Sessions

Session 0:   Abide 70 Expectations
Session 1:   Abide in the Gospel
Session 2:   Abide Alone with God
Session 3:   Worship
Session 4:   Abide by Boasting in Christ
Session 5:   Repentance, Renewal, and Rewiring
Session 6:   Abide in Christ's Perfection
Session 7:   Abide in Christ's Humility
Session 8:   Abide and Bear Much Fruit
Session 9:   Christ Pursued
Session 10:   Abide to the End

Permission to Love and Correct:

At the core of Abide70 is "giving permission" to other men to speak into your life. It involves vulnerability and allowing others to truly know you and correct you. This isn't about making legalistic standards for others, it is about holding your own life up to the truth of God's Word and allowing conviction to take root, giving your community of men the permission to hold you to the standards that you set for yourself because of those convictions. You will not hold yourself accountable—there is no such thing as self-accountability.

Session 0:
Abide70 Expectations

Why Abide: Christ is King

We have been trained by culture to believe that life, even a Christian life is about us: our needs, our wants. We emphasize is by asking questions like:

"Where do you think you will go if you die today?"

"How did you become saved?"

"Where are you finding your identity?"

"What is God's will for me?"

"What are your spiritual gifts?"

Or by making statements like:

"I need to process 'x'"

"Let me pray about it"

"God didn't tell me to do that"

In all of these very 'American Consumer Christianity' statements, 'I, you, and me' are very prominent, with no emphasis or expectation that submitting to God and his holy name and glory are needed.

For my name's sake I defer my anger; for the sake of my praise I restrain it for you, that I may not cut you off. behold, i have refined you, but not like silver; i have tried you in the furnace of affliction. for my own sake, i do it, for how should my name be profaned? my glory I will not give to another. (Isaiah 48:9-11)

Jesus Christ is King over everything. Everything.

The purpose of Abide70 is not to kick bad habits, lengthen the time between egregious sins or self-help. We were built for more than that. The purpose of developing rhythms that lead us to going deep in the word, close fellowship with other men, and denying ourselves is so <u>that we might know</u> the supreme God of the universe who holds all things together. To know God is to stand in awe of his Glory.

And this is eternal life, that they know you, the only true God, and Jesus Christ whom you have sent (John 17:3)

These things I have spoken to you, that my joy may be in you, and that your joy may be full. (John 15:11)

Therefore God has highly exalted him and bestowed on him the name that is above every name, so that at the name of Jesus every knee should bow, in heaven and on earth and under the earth, and every tongue confess that Jesus Christ is Lord, to the glory of God the Father. (Phillipians 2:9-11)

Abide70 is meant to challenge—it will be difficult, and that is good. It requires that you set aside time. You will have to participate in vulnerable discussions, you will be exposed. This may be the first time that you have been introduced to the spiritual disciplines. You may have deeply ingrained addictions and sins and habits that cling to you that you will need to cast aside. My prayer for you is that you embrace the challenge and for the next 70 days (and the rest of your life), to run with endurance and with passion the race that has been set before you for the sake of the supremacy and glory of God and joy of abiding in Jesus Christ–he has set the example for us.

Let us also lay aside every weight, and sin which clings so closely, and let us run with endurance the race that is set before us, looking to Jesus, the founder and perfecter of our faith, who for the joy that was set before him endured the cross, despising the shame, and is seated at the right hand of the throne of God. (Hebrews 12:1b-2)

John Piper preaches that followers of Christ should not simply ask what is permissible–that is the wrong question: we should ask–"does this activity help me to run for the glory of God?"

Can you answer that question honestly? Do you run for the glory of God? God is sovereign over all things. He is supreme over you, your sin, habits, routines, comforts, politics, health, entertainment, job, sexuality, marriage, singleness, parenting.

If you think that one thing escapes him, you are wrong–getting married is under his dominion. Watching youtube is under his dominion. Looking at yourself in the mirror is under his dominion. From the profound to the mundane, God has all authority and majesty and reigns over all things. This should fill us with awe.

Abraham Kuyper stated:

"There is not a square inch in the whole domain of our human existence over which Christ, who is Sovereign over all, does not cry, Mine!"

We need to have awareness of and affirm God's supreme ownership of our lives. We need to KNOW GOD by knowing Jesus Christ (John 17:3). One of the consequences of knowing God will be to stop coddling our sin and our comfort, and asking "is it actually a sin?" Another is turning outwards, forgetting ourselves, denying ourselves and selflessly serving others the way Jesus did, as the author and perfecter of our faith, he ran for the Glory of his Father (Hebrews 12:1-2) We start all of this by shedding our worldliness and all the burdens we bear, stop the striving for ourselves and our pleasures, and instead invest our time in energy in the things commanded of us in scripture. We need to put off our sin and put on Christ.

to put off your old self, which belongs to your former manner of life and is corrupt through deceitful desires, and to be renewed in the spirit of your minds, and to put on the new self, created after the likeness of God in true righteousness and holiness. (Ephesians 4:22-24)

Come to me, all who labor and are heavy laden, and I will give you rest. Take my yoke upon you, and learn from me, for I am gentle and lowly in heart, and you will find rest for your souls. (Matthew 11:28-29)

Let us rest in the supremacy and holiness of Christ together. Let us press on to know him more.

Let us know; let us press on to know the Lord;
his going out is sure as the dawn;
he will come to us as the showers,
as the spring rains that water the earth." (Hosea 6:3)

How to Abide: by Christ's Power

Seeking Christ and practicing the spiritual disciplines isn't a practice in teeth gritting self-discipline and stoicism. Without the "Why" (see above) we only are practicing self-discipline, self-love and self-help for our own selfish ends, <u>which is also a sin</u>. If you are in Christ, you have the Holy Spirit—and that Holy Spirit cannot abide with the practice of sin.

We have Christ in us, and he is now in charge of how we live.

I have been crucified with Christ. It is no longer I who live, but Christ who lives in me. And the life I now live in the flesh I live by faith in the Son of God, who loved me and gave himself for me. (Galatians 2:20)

Not by might, nor by power, but by my Spirit, says the Lord of hosts.
(Zechariah 4:6b)

By this we know that we abide in him and he in us, because he has given us of his Spirit. (1 John 4:13)

Therefore, my beloved, as you have always obeyed, so now, not only as in my presence but much more in my absence, work out your own salvation with fear and trembling, for it is

God who works in you, both to will and to work for his good pleasure. (Philippians 2:12-13)

God works in the believer–this is why we tremble: do you see your actions, your discipline, your daily activities as God "working in you?"

This is how God breaks the power of sin in us:

- Christ living through us (Galatians 2:20)
- By the Spirit (Zechariah 4:6b, 1 John 4:13)
- God working in us (Phillipians 2:12-13)

Let us shed the weight and sin we are carrying to run for God's glory. Brothers, let us press on to know him. Let this knowledge drive us to no longer practice sin, but practice and seek the righteousness of Christ. Let us abide in him.

Questions:

1. What do you want to get out of Abide70? In what ways do you want to grow?

2. Do you think that you are a Christian? What gives you assurance that you are?

3. Do you feel like you "know God (John 17:3)"? Are you running for the glory of God (Hebrews 12:1-2)? What weights and sins are hindering you from running?

4. "God is supreme over all things in my life." Do you agree or disagree? why? Is there any domain where you don't consider God "supreme"?

5. On a scale of 1-10, what level of victory do you feel you have over sin today? why?

6. What is your feeling about the spiritual disciplines? (reading the word, prayer, fasting, abstention from worldliness)

7. On a scale of 1-10 where would you say your practice of the spiritual disciplines is today?

8. "The spiritual disciplines are legalism—if I don't WANT to do them for the right reasons, I shouldn't do them at all": Do you agree or disagree with this statement? Why?

Session 1:
Abide in The Gospel

The Gospel

εὐαγγέλιον is the greek word for the gospel–in latin, it is the word evangelium, where we get the term "evangelical"--quite literally, it means "good news".

What is this good news?

You may have grown up in church and have heard it a thousand times, but we all still need to hear the gospel and live it every day. The following is excerpted from *"A Six-Point Summary of the Gospel | Desiring God"

> *1. God created us for his glory.*
>
> "Bring my sons from afar and my daughters from the end of the earth, everyone who is called by my name, whom I created for my glory" (Isaiah 43:6–7). God made all of us in his own image so that we would image forth, or reflect, his character and moral beauty.
>
> *2. Therefore every human should live for God's glory.*
>
> "Whether you eat or drink, or whatever you do, do all to the glory of God" (1 Corinthians 10:31). The way to live for the glory of God is to love him (Matthew 22:37), trust him (Romans 4:20), be thankful to him (Psalm 50:23), obey him (Matthew 5:16), and treasure

him above all things (Philippians 3:8; Matthew 10:37). When we do these things we image forth God's glory.

3. Nevertheless, we have all sinned and fallen short of God's glory.

"All have sinned and fall short of the glory of God" (Romans 3:23). "Although they knew God, they did not honor him as God or give thanks to him . . . and exchanged the glory of the immortal God for images" (Romans 1:21–23). None of us has loved or trusted or thanked or obeyed or treasured God as we ought.

4. Therefore we all deserve eternal punishment.

"The wages of sin is (eternal) death, but the free gift of God is eternal life in Christ Jesus our Lord" (Romans 6:23). Those who did not obey the Lord Jesus "will suffer the punishment of eternal destruction, away from the presence of the Lord and from the glory of his might" (2 Thessalonians 1:9). "These will go away into eternal punishment, but the righteous into eternal life" (Matthew 25:46).

5. Yet, in his great mercy, God sent his only Son Jesus Christ into the world to provide for sinners the way of eternal life.

"God so loved the world, that he gave his only Son, that whoever believes in him should not perish but have eternal life" (John 3:16). "Christ redeemed us from the curse of the law by becoming a curse for us"

(Galatians 3:13). "Christ also suffered once for sins, the righteous for the unrighteous, that he might bring us to God" (1 Peter 3:18).

6. Therefore eternal life is a free gift to all who will trust in Christ as Lord and Savior and supreme Treasure of their lives.

"Believe in the Lord Jesus, and you will be saved" (Acts 16:31). "If you confess with your mouth that Jesus is Lord and believe in your heart that God raised him from the dead, you will be saved" (Romans 10:9). "By grace you have been saved through faith. And this is not your own doing; it is the gift of God, not a result of works, so that no one may boast" (Ephesians 2:8–9). "I have been crucified with Christ. It is no longer I who live, but Christ who lives in me. And the life I now live in the flesh I live by faith in the Son of God, who loved me and gave himself for me" (Galatians 2:20). "I count everything as loss because of the surpassing worth of knowing Christ Jesus my Lord. For his sake I have suffered the loss of all things and count them as rubbish, in order that I may gain Christ" (Philippians 3:8).

---

https://www.desiringgod.org/articles/a-six-point-summary-of-the-gospel

When the truth of the Gospel becomes our hope, we overflow in obedience to Christ:

If you keep my commandments, you will abide in my love, just as I have kept my Father's commandments and abide in his love. (John 15:10).

When we abide in Christ, we point outward in mission, bearing fruit:

Abide in me, and I in you. As the branch cannot bear fruit by itself, unless it abides in the vine, neither can you, unless you abide in me. (John 15:4).

When we abide in Jesus we have the protection and provision of almighty God:

He who dwells in the shelter of the Most High
   will abide in the shadow of the Almighty. (Psalm 91:1)

We have nothing without abiding in Christ—we will not be able to conquer sin and work in power without his provision.

Spiritual Disciplines

(Take some time to read Resource: "The Spiritual Disciplines" by Don Whitney in appendix)

When it comes to practicing the spiritual disciplines we can, and we will, drift towards two main sins as Christian men—passivity or legalism. Our first father Adam's sin in the garden was passivity, and we are all stained by it. There is a passive attitude of "I don't want to do it as a checklist item" that we often use to support our laziness and to avoid spending time in prayer, reading scripture and worship. That passivity infects the way we lead our wives, our children and others–passivity is a path that always leads to ruin, death and hell.

The other sin that we will battle when it comes to the spiritual disciplines is legalism. We practice legalism when we set standards for others to follow paired with a condemning spirit when they don't achieve them. This unloving and is the path of self-righteousness and pride that also leads to ruin, death and hell.

We avoid these grave errors when we abide in the truth of the gospel. In the gospel we are freed to joyful obedience in Christ! Practicing the spiritual disciplines can help us in at least two ways:

1. The spiritual disciplines show us Jesus, leading to more joy in and reliance on him. Prayer, scripture reading, meditation on the word, worship, fasting and rest are all modeled and commanded at various points in scripture because they give us life. We go to Christ for our daily bread.

2. The spiritual disciplines provide us alternatives to other lesser pursuits: an hour in the word daily, an hour in prayer, 10 minutes meditating on a verse, actually fill us up: we are promised that the word of the Lord does not return void:

> *so shall my word be that goes out from my mouth;*
>   *it shall not return to me empty,*
> *but it shall accomplish that which I purpose,*
>   *and shall succeed in the thing for which I sent it. (Isaiah 55:11)*

When we are full of the things of the Lord, we don't binge watch, scroll, or seek the lesser sinful things—these things can't coexist in the same space because we have finite time, energy and bandwidth.

The spiritual disciplines have been practiced by Christians from the beginning of Christianity. By practicing the disciplines we follow in the long line of Christian brothers and sisters laying down their lives for Jesus. In practicing spiritual disciplines, we imitate Christ.

Practical Guardrails

One of practical aspects of Abide70 groups is to establish physical 'guardrails'. They are called guardrails because, like the steel rails on the side of a dangerous road, they provide a way to steer back to safety when we depart from the road of discipline. These take the form of dumbing down our phones, deleting social media, physical exercise, etc.. These guardrails don't prevent the sin or totally kill the sin that resides in each of our hearts, they simply make it more difficult to follow through with the act of sin, providing a barrier to remind us to 'steer to safety' when temptations inevitably come. These practical guardrails are Biblical:

For while bodily training is of some value, godliness is of value in every way, as it holds promise for the present life and also for the life to come. The saying is trustworthy and deserving of full acceptance. For to this end we toil and strive, because we have our hope set on the living God, who is the Savior of all people, especially of those who believe. (1 Timothy 4:8-10)

woe to the world for temptations to sin! For it is necessary that temptations come, but woe to the one by whom the temptation comes! and if your hand or your foot causes you to sin, cut it off and throw it away. It is better for you to enter life crippled or lame than with two hands or two feet to be thrown into the eternal fire. And if your eye causes you to sin, tear it out and throw it away. It is better for you to enter life with one eye than with two eyes to be thrown into the hell of fire. (Matthew 18:7-9)

It isn't legalism when we cut things out of our lives that are stepping stones toward sin. This is called obedience. If you find yourself scrolling facebook or looking at pornography habitually–why do you continue to have that opportunity? Why don't you have a guardrail in place? What does it look like to cut off your hand or tear out your eye? Satan wants you dead! Why would you give him a foothold?

Redeeming your time is important as well: when you establish a guardrail and cut something out–what do you replace it with? Maybe you listen to a popular politics (or sports or entertainment) podcast in the car that constantly sways you into thinking in worldly ways–replace it with a time in prayer, replace it with time in the word (there are audio Bibles), or time in worship. Maybe you watch a show that isn't honoring of God-replace it with Christian fellowship or hospitality-open up your space and host someone. It is a tragedy that we fill our days with things that do not stretch us and grow us to be more like Christ!

All of the above is for the sake of your soul. it is not meant to accuse or condemn you-it is not for the purposes of making you a joyless legalist-finding joy in purity and purpose instead of American mediocre lukewarm "christianity" will look different.

The gospel will transform you to new life.

The spiritual disciplines will grow your heart in and for Christ.

The practical guardrails, if done in Christ, will shut off the stream of inputs from a culture that is controlled by the prince of lies who wants you dead. Let us run this race together.

Questions:

1. Do you feel like you can articulate the Gospel?

2. Are there any aspects of the Gospel as articulated above that were new to you?

3. After a week, what spiritual disciplines are you practicing/trying to add to your life? Has it been a struggle? Where do you need to give permission to guys in this group to ask you about and call you out on?

4. What are your goals for growing in the gospel, practicing spiritual disciplines and practical guardrails as you start this journey? What truths of the Gospel do you need to push into more? What do you think will be the biggest obstacles for you to be engaged in Abide70?

5. How do the gospel and spiritual disciplines keep the physical guardrails from being the point of Abide70? Do you have a tendency to do the work of the guardrails without the heart of the gospel? How will you combat that tendency?

Session 2:
Abide Alone with God

Whoever says he abides in him ought to walk in the same way in which he walked. (1 John 2:6)

"...grant what you command, and command what you will."
Augustine of Hippo, Confessions X. xxix. trans. Henry Chadwick (Oxford 1991), p. 202.

Alone

While there is value in corporate worship, corporate accountability, corporate prayer, corporate scripture reading, etc, one of the key emphases of Abide70 is this: abiding alone with God. Without a practice of being alone with the Holy God of the universe, it is unlikely you will change into the man that he created you to be. When you kneel humbly alone in your room, and submit to the God of the universe there really is no formula for meeting with God, there is simply an attitude of humility.

"I need you."
"I need you."
"I need you."

We cannot do anything apart from Jesus. We need him. He is God incarnate whose sacrifice on the cross to atone for our sins is sufficient! He has victory over sin and death, so a practice of daily, hourly, constant meeting with God is necessary. We do not meet with God as a means to appease him. He does not need our worship, money or prayer.

The God who made the world and everything in it, being Lord of heaven and earth, does not live in temples made by man, nor is he served by human hands, as though he needed anything, since he himself gives to all mankind life and breath and everything (Acts 17:24-25)

He is the image of the invisible God, the firstborn of all creation. For by him all things were created, in heaven and on earth, visible and invisible, whether thrones or dominions or rulers or authorities—all things were created through him and for him. And he is before all things, and in him all things hold together. And he is the head of the body, the church. He is the beginning, the firstborn from the dead, that in everything he might be preeminent. For in him all the fullness of God was pleased to dwell, and through him to reconcile to himself all things, whether on earth or in heaven, making peace by the blood of his cross. (Colossians 3:15-20)

Because of Christ, we have access to God the Father, we get to enter into the throne room of grace.

Therefore, since we have been justified by faith, we have peace with God through our Lord Jesus Christ. Through him we have also obtained access by faith into this grace in which we stand, and we rejoice in hope of the glory of God. (Romans 5:1-2)

Brothers, let us not neglect this great gift—let us meet with the Father just as Jesus often did (Mark 1:35, Luke 4:42, Matthew 14:13, Matthew 14:23, John 6:15, Luke 5:16).

We have to plan and prepare to meet with God—it is imperative that we reorient our schedule to meet with him, but we cannot depend on our heart to want to do it—because it is desperately wicked (Jeremiah 17:9). Build a plan.

Plan: When, Where, How

When: set aside a time to pray and read scripture, this is easier if it is part of a routine or habit. Because we have examples of a practice of morning meeting with God, as well as the practicality of starting the day out right, morning is the ideal time, particularly before the rest of the family wakes. If for some reason, this doesn't work for you, pick a specific dedicated time to pray, read scripture, sing hymns, and tell other brothers when that time is, so that they can hold you accountable.

Where: in some versions of the Bible a "prayer closet" is mentioned in Matthew 6:5-6. This has caused some confusion—a prayer closet is simply a "desolate place" like where Jesus went to meet with his Father. If you are the first one up in the mornings, it may be your kitchen table. If your house is full of screaming kids or roommates, you may need to go to a park, or your backyard, and yes, it might even be a closet in your house. Find a regular, separate space where you can meet alone with God, where there is no distraction and no electronic device!

How: Not everyone is the same—some of us would like some soft worship music to prepare us for a time of worship, others prepare by having a hymnal or a guitar on hand. A Bible is a must, and maybe you like to highlight or journal and have a prayer list so you can pray in a focused way. There is no specific prescription for what our time alone with God has to look like, but we should be growing in our practice of feeding on the Word of God, longing for his kingdom, worshiping him, and relying on him for our daily providence and resistance to sin. I have found much value in talking to other brothers about what works for them. I encourage you to ask others about their practices, and share about your own. The main thing here is to just do it—over and over. Day by day. If you miss a day, don't miss two. Even if you feel like it is fruitless, it is in the disciplined, regular, day by day practice that we grow.

Prepare: Ask for Heart Change.

One of the wisest people I know (my wife) has given this advice "do what is right—and ask for the heart", which echos very strongly of Augustine, quoted above: obedience is an act of the will, and while we would love for every act of obedience to flow from pure desire to glorify God, we know that many times, the God-given fruit and grace of self-discipline and is in order.

God is the only one that changes hearts, changes tastebuds, changes eyes to see and ears to hear.

Our excuses are plentiful—if you have ever used one of the following phrases for not meeting alone with God (or practicing the other spiritual disciplines), you have company!

"I don't want to do it for the wrong reasons"
"If I am not doing it joyfully, I don't want to do it"

"I don't want to be legalistic"
"I just don't feel like it"
"I need to pray about it, it might not be for me"
"It isn't my personality, I am not a reader/prayer/singer, etc."
"I need to process this first."

I have used them—but they are wrong. Satan would use these as reasons to keep us from obeying—we are commanded to pray alone (Matthew 6:6) and we are given plenty of examples in scripture—our feelings and experience cannot be the dictate of what we do—if we know the word and the commands, we need to conform to the will of God, then plead earnestly to the Lord for the heart to do it—and he will:

"Ask, and it will be given to you; seek, and you will find; knock, and it will be opened to you. For everyone who asks receives, and the one who seeks finds, and to the one who knocks it will be opened. Or which one of you, if his son asks him for bread, will give him a stone? Or if he asks for a fish, will give him a serpent? If you then, who are evil, know how to give good gifts to your children, how much more will your Father who is in heaven give good things to those who ask him! (Matthew 7:7-11)

If you abide in me, and my words abide in you, ask whatever you wish, and it will be done for you. (John 15:7)

God doesn't give us a timetable for this—for giving us the "want to" and the joy in obedience: he just promises that he will do it. It is perhaps the suffering that we do in the practice of self-discipline, giving up more desirable and pleasurable things that God is refining us for his Glory.

Why do we spend time in the Bible instead of another book or devotional? Because the Bible is the main, promised way that we hear God speak: the Gideons—who place Bibles in hotel rooms across the country have this intro in each of the bibles they place:

"The Bible contains the mind of God, the state of man, the way of salvation, the doom of sinners, and the happiness of believers.

Its doctrines are holy, its precepts are binding, its histories are true, and its decisions are immutable.

Read it to be wise, believe it to be safe, and practice it to be holy.

It contains light to direct you, food to support you, and comfort to cheer you.

It is the traveler's map, the pilgrim's staff, the pilot's compass, the soldier's sword and the Christian's charter.

Here too, Heaven is opened and the gates of Hell disclosed.

Christ is its grand subject, our good its design, and the glory of God its end.

It should fill the memory, rule the heart, and guide the feet.

Read it slowly, frequently, and prayerfully.

It is a mine of wealth, a paradise of glory, and a river of pleasure.

It is given you in life, will be opened at the judgment, and be remembered forever.

It involves the highest responsibility, rewards the greatest labor, and will condemn all who trifle with its sacred contents."

God's word does not return void. (Isaiah 55:11) I have heard joyless but disciplined time in the word spoken about like this:

Our joyless self-discipline of prayer and time in the word may be drudgery, seemingly joyless, but it is like putting dry kindling in a fire pit.

we pile it on.
we pile it on.
we pile it on.

And nothing happens. One day, God sends the fire, the spark of the Holy Spirit and ignites the dry kindling. Putting the dry kindling was not an act of futility. The words that we read and felt nothing are now alive and breathing and we have access to them, and they have power! Holy Spirit power!

If we cannot meet with God and it be a joyful practice, let us do the work of splitting the kindling, adding it to the fire ring, then crying out to the Lord to send the fire of the Holy Spirit and ignite our hearts, and in doing it, he will give us himself, and, it will become the joy of our hearts to be in the presence of God!

Questions:

1. Do you have a regular practice of private time in the word? Of Prayer? Of Worship? Where do you think you are the weakest? Do you have a "prayer closet"? How can your brothers encourage you in the practice of abiding alone in God?

2. What excuses keep you from being in the word? What permission do you need to give to others to ask about your time in the word? What stops you from challenging others from being in the word (even when you are not)?

3. Do you agree with the "kindling" metaphor above? Why or why not?

4. Are you a patient person? How long do you think you need to "wait on the Lord" before he responds?

5. "Do the right thing—and ask for the heart" Do you agree with this? Are there biblical reasons to disagree?

6. Do you have a practice of scripture memorization? Why not? How can others challenge you in memorizing more scripture so that you can abide without having a Bible?

Session 3:
Worship

We have spent much time talking about cutting away wasted time and energy, fleeing from sin, but we haven't spent much time talking about "running towards": and in Christ, we have an example:

Therefore, since we are surrounded by so great a cloud of witnesses, let us also lay aside every weight, and sin which clings so closely, and let us run with endurance the race that is set before us, looking to Jesus, the founder and perfecter of our faith, who for the joy that was set before him endured the cross, despising the shame, and is seated at the right hand of the throne of God. (Hebrews 12:1-2)

Why did Christ suffer? Why did he endure the cross? For the JOY that was set before him! Oh that we would run—not just from sin, but that we would run to the Father who offers us endless and infinite joy!

Our senses are dulled to it, but Christ does not tell us to put away happiness and joy, he tells us to seek it in him:

"The kingdom of heaven is like treasure hidden in a field, which a man found and covered up. Then in his joy he goes and sells all that he has and buys that field. (Matthew 13:44)

You see? We think we give something up to pursue Christ, but we get infinitely more! Jonathan Edwards knew this—he talked of the affections, that which stirs us for the things of Christ! What is it that causes you to cry out to God—Abba!

Father? Are you dumbfounded with gratefulness and joy for your salvation? My pastor often says from the pulpit "You cannot worship a God you do not know" and this is certainly true–if we do not know him, if our affections are not stirred, if we are not happy in Christ, how will we worship him? We must know him more!

Worship is Personal

We covered this in the last session, "Abide Alone with God" . We get the opportunity to enter the throne room–Jesus has made away–don't neglect to rest in the presence of God!

You will show me the path of life;
In Your presence is fullness of joy;
At Your right hand are pleasures forevermore.(Psalm 16:11)

Worship is Corporate

And let us consider how to stir up one another to love and good works, not neglecting to meet together, as is the habit of some, but encouraging one another, and all the more as you see the Day drawing near. (Hebrews 10:24-25)

Let us not fail to meet with the body in worship–this is where we get to encourage one another with hands lifted high in worship of the Father!

Our Worship is Obedience

I appeal to you therefore, brothers, by the mercies of God, to present your bodies as a living sacrifice, holy and acceptable to God, which is your spiritual worship. (Hebrews 12:1)

Worship is obedience and laying down our lives for others, for the sake of pointing to God's perfect sacrifice of his son!

Worship is Eternal

One truth about worship is that it is something that we get to participate in today, tomorrow and forever–it is a taste of what we will participate in when we are in heaven with Christ!

But the hour is coming, and is now here, when the true worshipers will worship the Father in spirit and truth, for the Father is seeking such people to worship him. (John 4:23)

And I heard every creature in heaven and on earth and under the earth and in the sea, and all that is in them, saying,

*"To him who sits on the throne and to the Lamb
be blessing and honor and glory and might forever and ever!"
(Revelation 5:13)*

We were made to worship God, we were created for his glory. As question 1 of the Westminster Catechism puts it:

Q. 1. *What is the chief end of man?*

A. *Man's chief end is to glorify God, and to enjoy him forever.*

Practically, how will this play out in our lives?

Gratitude

We are commanded to give thanks.

Oh give thanks to the LORD, for he is good;

for his steadfast love endures forever! (1 Chronicles 16:34)

Praise the LORD!
Oh give thanks to the LORD, for he is good,
for his steadfast love endures forever! (Psalm 106:1)

Thanksgiving requires assessment: we do not stop and think about the providence of the Lord for our salvation, for physical blessing, for spiritual blessing—we are tuned to our culture, always feeling a pull towards materialism and consumerism, feeling that we are "less than" if we do not have the next _____ fill in the blank. Let us worship the God who gives us life and breath and everything! Let us worship him for drawing us to himself and not abandoning us to ourselves.

Contentment

For the sake of Christ, then, I am content with weaknesses, insults, hardships, persecutions, and calamities. For when I am weak, then I am strong. (2 Corinthians 12:10)

Not that I am speaking of being in need, for I have learned in whatever situation I am to be content. (Phillipians 4:11)

But if we have food and clothing, with these we will be content. (1 Timothy 6:8)

Keep your life free from love of money, and be content with what you have, for he has said, "I will never leave you nor forsake you." (Hebrews 13:5)

Do all things without grumbling or disputing, that you may be blameless and innocent, children of God without blemish in the midst of a crooked and twisted generation, among whom you shine as lights in the world, (Phillipans 2:14-15)

I confess that I struggle so much with this command. I grumble and complain, and even if I do not do it outwardly, I do it in my joyless attitude. We are commanded to thank God and be content with what we have—even if it is calamity and insults and hardship, finding satisfaction in Christ, and agreeing with his sovereignty in what he has blessed us with.

Enjoyment and Idols

Contentment isn't just "making do with what we have", but joyful celebration—God gives us good gifts!

Every good gift and every perfect gift is from above, coming down from the Father of lights, with whom there is no variation or shadow due to change (James 1:17)

Behold, what I have seen to be good and fitting is to eat and drink and find enjoyment in all the toil with which one toils under the sun the few days of his life that God has given him, for this is his lot. Everyone also to whom God has given wealth and possessions and power to enjoy them, and to accept his lot and rejoice in his toil—this is the gift of God. For he will not much remember the days of his life because God keeps him occupied with joy in his heart. (Ecclesiastes 5:18-20)

Let your fountain be blessed,

and rejoice in the wife of your youth, (Proverbs 5:18)

And you shall rejoice in all the good that the LORD your God has given to you and to your house, you, and the Levite, and the sojourner who is among you. (Deuteronomy 14:26)

We are not to make idols of any of these enjoyments as we are prone to do. We are to give generously of the gifts that God has stewarded to us (Luke 12:48b)–this is also worship.

Fear but Comfort

Are you in awe of, in fear of God? Just as we should ask for gratitude, ask for contentment, ask for enjoyment, we are to ask for more fear, more awe of the Lord–when we see him as he is, we fall down in worship. Following are several examples of men of faith who were awed by the holiness of God:

Isaiah
In the year that King Uzziah died I saw the Lord sitting upon a throne, high and lifted up; and the train of his robe filled the temple. Above him stood the seraphim. Each had six wings: with two he covered his face, and with two he covered his feet, and with two he flew. And one called to another and said: "Holy, holy, holy is the Lord of hosts;
the whole earth is full of his glory!"
And the foundations of the thresholds shook at the voice of him who called, and the house was filled with smoke. And I said: "Woe is me! For I am lost; for I am a man of unclean lips, and I dwell in the midst of a people of unclean lips; for my eyes have seen the King, the Lord of hosts!"

Then one of the seraphim flew to me, having in his hand a burning coal that he had taken with tongs from the altar. And he touched my mouth and said: "Behold, this has touched your lips; your guilt is taken away, and your sin atoned for." (Isaiah 6:1-7)

Daniel
So I was left alone and saw this great vision, and no strength was left in me. My radiant appearance was fearfully changed, and I retained no strength. Then I heard the sound of his words, and as I heard the sound of his words, I fell on my face in deep sleep with my face to the ground.

And behold, a hand touched me and set me trembling on my hands and knees. And he said to me, "O Daniel, man greatly loved, understand the words that I speak to you, and stand upright, for now I have been sent to you." And when he had spoken this word to me, I stood up trembling. Then he said to me, "Fear not, Daniel, for from the first day that you set your heart to understand and humbled yourself before your God, your words have been heard, and I have come because of your words (Daniel 10:8-12)

Peter
But when Simon Peter saw it, he fell down at Jesus' knees, saying, "Depart from me, for I am a sinful man, O Lord." (Luke 5:8)

John
Then I turned to see the voice that was speaking to me, and on turning I saw seven golden lampstands, and in the midst of the lampstands one like a son of man, clothed with a long

robe and with a golden sash around his chest. The hairs of his head were white, like white wool, like snow. His eyes were like a flame of fire, his feet were like burnished bronze, refined in a furnace, and his voice was like the roar of many waters. In his right hand he held seven stars, from his mouth came a sharp two-edged sword, and his face was like the sun shining in full strength.
When I saw him, I fell at his feet as though dead. But he laid his right hand on me, saying, "Fear not, I am the first and the last, and the living one. I died, and behold I am alive forevermore, and I have the keys of Death and Hades. (Revelation 1:12-18)

Every time that God appears in these scenarios, he restores—he cleanses Isaiah and takes away his guilt, he touches Daniel, he calls Peter to follow him. He lays his right hand upon John and comforts him.

Jesus does not comfort them with the comfort of food, or sex, drugs, or entertainment. He gives them the comfort of himself.

Come to me, all who labor and are heavy laden, and I will give you rest. (Matthew 11:28)

Comfort and rest don't come without a condition:

Take my yoke upon you, and learn from me, for I am gentle and lowly in heart, and you will find rest for your souls. For my yoke is easy, and my burden is light. (Matthew 11:29-30) to put off your old self, which belongs to your former manner of life and is corrupt through deceitful desires, and to be renewed in the spirit of your minds, and to put on the new self, created after the likeness of God in true righteousness and holiness. (Ephesians 4:22-24)

There is a taking up a yoke, and a taking off of the sin and flesh. There is also a putting on, of the truth of the gospel, of a reliance on Christ, of a joyful obedience, of our identity in Christ. Obedience leads to joy, and joy leads to obedience!

Christ wants us to enter the throne room boldly, because he makes a way despite our sin and shame to enter his Holy Presence. Let worship be the reason why we run from sin, let worship be why we run to him—he will comfort us with his presence and we will join the chorus of the saints for all time who proclaim:

To him who sits on the throne and to the Lamb
be blessing and honor and glory and might forever and ever!
(Revelation 5:13b)

Questions:

1. What do you find it easier to do—obey dutifully, or worship out of pure desire to worship?

2. What stirs your affections for the things for God, what causes you to worship?

3. Where do you need to give others permission to keep you accountable to seeking regular times of worship?

4. What obstacles keep you from worshiping? What hinders your gratitude and contentment?

5. What Idols are you most likely to worship? Do you find that they are the same as the obstacles?

6. "My lack of worship coincides with an increase in my sin." Is this statement true of you? Why or why not?

7. "Others seem like they are better at worshiping than me" Is this a lie you hear? Where does it cause you to go for your comfort?

Session 4:
Abide by Boasting in Christ

But he said to me, "My grace is sufficient for you, for my power is made perfect in weakness." Therefore I will boast all the more gladly of my weaknesses, so that the power of Christ may rest upon me. For the sake of Christ, then, I am content with weaknesses, insults, hardships, persecutions, and calamities. For when I am weak, then I am strong. (2 Corinthians 12:9-10)

Therefore, since we have been justified by faith, we have peace with God through our Lord Jesus Christ. Through him we have also obtained access by faith into this grace in which we stand, and we rejoice in hope of the glory of God (Romans 5:1-2)

Peace with God

Do you feel you are at peace with God? If you are in Christ, no matter what you have done, or how far you have strayed, or how you feel, he is calling you back to himself. You have the Holy Spirit, Christ in you who is always there. As sinners, we have a tendency to feel like we must confess <u>in order to earn</u> our place in the arms of Jesus, but the fact is, he already made peace for us if we believed on him.

For in him all the fullness of God was pleased to dwell, and through him to reconcile to himself all things, whether on earth or in heaven, making peace by the blood of his cross. (Colossians 1:19-20)

Justification, our position and peace in Christ is not affected by confession, but if we live in unrepentant sin, we will grieve the Holy Spirit.

And do not grieve the Holy Spirit of God, by whom you were sealed for the day of redemption. (Ephesians 4:30)

One who is positionally at peace with God will desire to confess their sin regularly, and will ask for God to search them:

Search me, O God, and know my heart!
   Try me and know my thoughts
And see if there be any grievous way in me,
   and lead me in the way everlasting! (Psalm 139:23-24)
If we are given peace with God, let us live in that peace with him through a true heart of confession!

Professional Confession vs. Asking for Intercession

Some Christians have become "professional confessors" to one another: those who have become so good at confessing because of the attention that they receive.
Assess:
- Am I confessing because I think that confession to man makes me right with God?
- Am I confessing because I want to be affirmed that I am not the only one struggling?
- Am I confessing because I want attention, to be coddled?
- or:

- Am I confessing because I am in desperate need of Christ's nearness?
- Am I confessing because I want other brothers to come around me, intercede for me and remind me of the Gospel?

When we speak to our brothers of our weaknesses, faults and sins that we still battle, let us trust in Christ's forgiveness, and ask for intercession and encouragement to endure the battle! If I am a hearer of confession, assess:
- Do I feel better about my own sin and justify it when someone confesses theirs?
- Do I coddle the confessor, and "let them off the hook?"
- Do I build up the confessor's self esteem and their ability to "get right with God?"
or:
- Do I acknowledge their sin, remind them of the Gospel and intercede for them?
- Do I long for others to live out their peace with God?

We confess for healing and strength for the continuing battle:

Therefore, confess your sins to one another and pray for one another, that you may be healed. The prayer of a righteous person has great power as it is working (James 5:16)

So that we can bear one another's burdens:

Bear one another's burdens, and so fulfill the law of Christ. (Galatians 6:2)

So that we can restore one another in gentleness:

Brothers, if anyone is caught in any transgression, you who are spiritual should restore him in a spirit of gentleness. Keep watch on yourself, lest you too be tempted. (Galatians 6:1)

Stories of weakness are a reminder that we are also weak–and we trust in God to provide us strength for the battle.

If you are an unbeliever, live in unconfessed, unrepentant sin before God, run to him. Confess to him. Put your trust in him alone! Don't trust your confession, trust Jesus, he is the peacemaker!

If we confess our sins, he is faithful and just to forgive us our sins and to cleanse us from all unrighteousness. (1 John 1:9)

If you are a believer, vulnerability with your sins and weaknesses is an opportunity to restore and be restored in gentleness!

Testimony

So what do we do with sin now? A posture of confessing where we have been weak and how God has overcome with his strength and the blood of Jesus, how he has restored us, should always be on our lips as we talk to believers and unbelievers. Allowing others to see how miserably weak we continue to be despite our right relationship with God is a testimony to God's faithfulness amidst our failures. This is how we overcome the "be a good person" myth that is so pervasive in both Christian and non-Christian circles.

How do we know we are alive in Christ? Pastor John Piper says that we do not show our proof of life by showing our people our birth certificate—we show them by breathing.

Similarly, we don't show others we are a believer by pointing to an event that happened in the past, or our baptism, we breathe, we live, we boast in what Christ is doing in us now in our weakness—this is our testimony. We often think of a testimony as something that happened to us in the past—how we came to first know Christ, and while that is a part of our testimony, we need to press into how God is working in us and through us now, transforming us from one degree of glory to another—this is how we boast in the excellencies of God NOW.

Testimonies are powerful, and I have witnessed firsthand how testimonies change the trajectory of lives and marriages and generations—boast in Christ! Your testimony is how God is showing you right now who he is. If you have not rehearsed it and regularly speak of how God is healing and working in you now, spend time considering where and to whom you could be speaking your testimony.

Questions:

1. What is your testimony—how do you boast in what Christ is doing in you today? Write down your testimony and be ready to share.

2. Have you ever confessed sin to someone, only to receive condemnation? How has that bad experience with confession influenced how/who you confess to today?

3. Do you have one "closer than a brother"(Proverbs 18:24) who you can be completely open and honest with, someone who knows you and you can confess sin to and will point you to Christ?

4. Are you dealing with any unconfessed secret sin right now? Confess it to your Abide70 group.

5. Look at the questions on page 51-52–do any of these characterize your confession (good or bad) or your attitude as one who is being confessed to (good or bad)?

Session 5:
Repentance, Renewal and Rewiring

Repentance

For I consider that the sufferings of this present time are not worth comparing with the glory that is to be revealed to us. For the creation waits with eager longing for the revealing of the sons of God. For the creation was subjected to futility, not willingly, but because of him who subjected it, in hope that the creation itself will be set free from its bondage to corruption and obtain the freedom of the glory of the children of God. For we know that the whole creation has been groaning together in the pains of childbirth until now. And not only the creation, but we ourselves, who have the firstfruits of the Spirit, groan inwardly as we wait eagerly for adoption as sons, the redemption of our bodies. (Romans 8:18-23)

Confession is not the end. It is the beginning. To repent (μετανοέω/metanoéō) is to change, turn back from—it is a conscious act of the will to obey and run from. God IS absolutely sovereign in all things, and yet, we are told to obey:

Flee from sexual immorality. Every other sin a person commits is outside the body, but the sexually immoral person sins against his own body. (1 Corinthians 6:18)

Rejoice in the Lord always; again I will say, rejoice. (Phillipians 4:4)

Repent, for the kingdom of heaven is at hand. (Matthew 3:2) work out your own salvation with fear and trembling (Philliipians 2:12b)

Flee! Rejoice! Repent! Work!
These are commands, and we are to submit ourselves to them—but doesn't that sound like the law? Isn't that legalism? No, because this obedience does not come from us—it comes from God—we see this in the broader context of the last verse—

work out your own salvation with fear and trembling, for it is God who works in you, both to will and to work for his good pleasure. (Philippians 2:12b-13 emphasis added)

How do we work? Why do we tremble? Because an infinite God compels you, controls you! You are in awe of the work he is doing through and for you!

For the love of Christ controls us, because we have concluded this: that one has died for all, therefore all have died; and he died for all, that those who live might no longer live for themselves but for him who for their sake died and was raised. (2 Corinthians 5:14-15)

I have been crucified with Christ. It is no longer I who live but Crhist who lives in me. And the life I now live in the flesh I live by faith in the Son of God who loved me and gave himself for me (Galatians 2:20)

When we repent and turn from sin, change is possible because it is no longer you and I working in our own power, it is Jesus who is working. Evidence of turning from sin is action oriented: having an action plan for steps you will take is the fruit of repentance that has taken root—if you are in a season of repenting from sin, show your work: make a plan and share it with others who will hold you accountable to it.

Renewal

There is therefore now no condemnation for those who are in Christ Jesus. (Romans 8:1)

Therefore, if anyone is in Christ, he is a new creation. The old has passed away; behold, the new has come. (2 Corinthians 5:17)

"Come now, let us reason together, says the Lord: though your sins are like scarlet, they shall be as white as snow; though they are red like crimson, they shall become like wool. (Isaiah 1:18)

And I will give you a new heart, and a new spirit I will put within you. And I will remove the heart of stone from your flesh and give you a heart of flesh. And I will put my Spirit within you, and cause you to walk in my statutes and be careful to obey my rules (Ezekiel 36:26-27)

If you have confessed faith in Jesus and put your hope in Jesus Christ's life, death and resurrection, you are new! Each day, live into that newness: we have the Holy Spirit, we have resurrection power! Though it is our story that Christ triumphed over our sin, sin is not our identity—let Christ complete the story—that he is the one that is alive in us, and that we are made new in Him. If this is true, each day, we open our eyes to the new mercies of Christ! We awake in our new identity! Take time to soak in the truth of Romans 6:

What shall we say then? Are we to continue in sin that grace may abound? By no means! How can we who died to sin still live in it? Do you not know that all of us who have been baptized into Christ Jesus were baptized into his death? We were buried therefore with him by baptism into death, in order that, just as Christ was raised from the dead by the glory of the Father, we too might walk in newness of life.

For if we have been united with him in a death like his, we shall certainly be united with him in a resurrection like his. We know that our old self was crucified with him in order that the body of sin might be brought to nothing, so that we would no longer be enslaved to sin. For one who has died has been set free from sin. Now if we have died with Christ, we believe that we will also live with him. We know that Christ, being raised from the dead, will never die again; death no longer has dominion over him. For the death he died he died to sin, once for all, but the life he lives he lives to God. So you also must consider yourselves dead to sin and alive to God in Christ Jesus.

Let not sin therefore reign in your mortal body, to make you obey its passions. Do not present your members to sin as instruments for unrighteousness, but present yourselves to God as those who have been brought from death to life, and your members to God as instruments for righteousness. For sin will have no dominion over you, since you are not under law but under grace. (Romans 6:1-14)

Saturate in this truth—you have been made new.

Do not fall into the trap of not believing the truth that if you come to the feet of Christ with your sin, YOU ARE FORGIVEN. Your forgiveness is not based on your feelings. If you have confessed and are participating in the work of repentance, you are pure, you have been washed clean. Don't commit the new sin of pride and arrogance and unbelief that God's word doesn't mean what it says.

Christ is coming again, and he will complete the work in you:

And I am sure of this, that he who began a good work in you will bring it to completion at the day of Jesus Christ. (Philippians 1:6)

Yes, we groan, and we battle—but it is because we have begun the process of transforming, and we will be made like Christ in the end! We are being renewed and sanctified and glorified in Christ.

Rewiring from Worldliness

Our minds, like our bodies, are broken, and our flesh still is drawn to sin and death. Unfortunately, the dopamine hits of pornography and games and entertainment and passivity and laziness and comfort and substances has done a number on our brains and bodies. "Old habits die hard" they say, and it is true—once we have established patterns in our brains, we have created pathways of sin that want to stay open. We want to think of "our spiritual self" and "our physical self" but they are so interwoven and connected—this is why God places so much emphasis on the importance of caring for our bodies, in this world, they will die an earthly death, but they will also be made new one day. There is much scientific literature out there to tell us the physical and mental consequences of the sins that we commit, and we also know that scripture tells us we are fighting a battle that goes beyond flesh and blood.

For we do not wrestle against flesh and blood, but against the rulers, against the authorities, against the cosmic powers over this present darkness, against the spiritual forces of evil in the heavenly place. (Ephesians 6:12)

Satan is in league with those who control the marketing algorithms which guide our lives to conquer men using our God-given biology. Our consumer culture takes advantage of the sins of our flesh: lust, insecurity, anxiety about the future to conquer us into spending more money: "Just Do It". "Have it Your Way". "Bet you can't just eat one". "The best a man can get". Sex sells, and we are buying it.

The physical consequences of sexual, substance, gambling or entertainment-induced sin last for a long time–and you have to be committed to the process of rewiring. Satan wants you dead and hates that you want to change.

You can change.

Discipline, accountability, patience, are helpful, but Holy Spirit is required: By his power, you can put off the darkness that you once walked in, and in the light, pursue your new love, Jesus Christ. If he is not your light, aim or love, you are destined to forever be enslaved to your flesh.

Rewiring is radical—it involves hand cutting and eye-gouging. The following is a practical list that men I know have undertaken in order to rewire radically—the men I know who have done these things and have been successful have had the motivation of seeking Christ first as the 'why' behind pursuing these rewiring efforts. None of these efforts remove your desire to sin, nor do they remove your ability to sin. Seeking Christ first is what will overcome your sin.

- Replacing a smartphone with a dumbphone, or practically making your smartphone a dumbphone, giving your wife or friends full access of the activities you pursue with it.
- Deleting any dating or any type of app that would give you access to a sinful outlet.
- Deleting social media, shopping apps, games anything distracting on your phone
- Not going to places where there will be temptation (the pool, the beach, the gym)
- Deleting and selling (or destroying) video games
- Limiting, even eliminating "non-business use" of internet at home
- Deleting entertainment—Netflix, Disney+ etc., drastically reducing or eliminating tv/movie watching.
- No phone in the bathroom, etc.

These are just examples, be thoughtful—if your initial inclination is "but I need a phone to do work" or "I can't do that…" or "It is helpful for….." know that <u>I am not putting any burden upon you</u>—this is your choice. Ask yourself "am I really making excuses so that I can pursue my sin?" or are you actually seeking the Lord and can say that you are earnestly practicing gouging out eyes and cutting off hands in order to pursue purity and righteousness? You know what YOU need to do—if you are convicted about the way you interact with your phone, entertainment and the world, talk to one of your trusted brothers—(see "Give Someone the Keys") below.

Numerous books have been written about the actual process of detoxing from the neurological effects of sin and addiction—and many people trying to disconnect from their sin spend much time looking at the science and trying to understand it. While it may be interesting, and sometimes is helpful to know what is going on in the black box of your brain, it can be a distraction and an excuse that leads to continued walking in disobedience, because it doesn't go to the root of the issue. Spend more time in scripture and prayer than on books about how hard addiction is to break.

Rewiring does not look like the world. Rewiring may be embarrassing or inconvenient. Rewiring is weird, but it may save your life, your marriage, your family, your soul. Jesus said things that offended and enraged others—are you willing to follow him and obey? What is he calling you to?

Moderation

Maybe you can "play a few games", "watch a few youtube videos", "scroll a few minutes on facebook" but when does that cross the line into "watch a little porn", "cheat a little", "lie a little" Maybe you can see the lines, but your brain's chemicals do not know the differences. "Moderation in everything" is a lie and a buzzword that means "a little sinning never hurt anyone" but you know that it does hurt people. It hurts and kills you and others around you to the core. If scrolling late at night always leads to pornography, you have to understand what started you down that journey, and not moderate it, but completely change the root behaviors.

But sexual immorality and all impurity or covetousness must not even be named among you, as is proper among saints. Let there be no filthiness nor foolish talk nor crude joking, which are out of place, but instead let there be thanksgiving. (Ephesians 5:3-4)

Think about the men you most look up to: men who are 'all in' are rarely moderate, they are principled, and have disciplines in place to help them to pursue Christ and flee from sin. These men do not have stronger willpower than you, they simply have done a better job at eliminating choices that are going to lead them down the path of failure. Real freedom means making the decision to not have the choice whether to pursue something that enslaves you or not.

Give Someone the Keys

Like someone making the decision before drinking to hand over the keys to a designated driver (I understand the irony of this example for Abide70, but bear with me), we should be giving someone else the keys when it comes to decisions where we may be impaired by bias, addiction or inclination:

A man who is dating is impaired by infatuation and the allure of a girlfriend should have wise counsel when he is seeking marriage or engagement. He should hand over the keys—have wise and biblical men telling him if it is a good idea to continue to pursue—and he should listen and obey them if they determine it isn't a good time to continue dating or a good match (unequally yoked or other Biblical reason not to marry.)

A man who is addicted to pornography or games is impaired by addiction, comfort and pleasure. He should hand over the keys—have his history and permissions sent to a wise and trusted man or group of men—someone who will ask questions and not "let them off the hook". Someone who will call him to MORE, to ask him if he has gone far enough in his "eye-gouging" when he falls into sin.

Christ calls us to love him above all our other loves.

Obedience From the Overflow

While the cutting away is helpful, ultimately, none of it will be effective if we are not living out of the overflow of worship of Christ, love of Christ, running to and trusting in Christ—when we abide Jesus, we stand under the waterfall of grace and

We cut away and rewire so that we might better stand in that place—we cut away so that we might remove the distraction so that we might receive and give the grace that God supplies!

David Mathis says that: "Christian self-control is not finally about bringing our bodily passions under our own control, but under the control of Christ by the power of his Spirit."

For the love of Christ controls us, because we have concluded this: that one has died for all, therefore all have died; and he died for all, that those who live might no longer live for themselves but for him who for their sake died and was raised. (2 Corinthians 5:14-15)

A man without self-control
   is like a city broken into and left without walls.
(Proverbs 25:28)

Christ calls us to repentance. Only when we repent can we experience a renewal and a desire for complete transformation: then we will make a plan to rewire so that we might better glorify the Lord in our bodies.

Questions:

1. What repentance are you putting off? Do you believe you cannot be forgiven? Why?

2. Do you agree that obedience is work?

3. What would it look like for you to rewire? What barriers do you know would be helpful but you refuse to do? Is it because you love your comfort more Christ? Or another reason?–(give the reason and see if it flies with the guys you have as accountability partners-)

4. Ask yourself, and then another who knows you well "what am I impaired by?" and don't be defensive. You may not like what you hear—do you have a sense for what you think you may be impaired by and need to "give someone else the keys?"

5. Obedience is from the overflow: how does this play out in your life as you seek to follow Christ?

6. What activities stir your affections for the things of God? How might you better incorporate these into your life?

Session 6:
Abide in Christ's Perfection

And we all, with unveiled face, beholding the glory of the Lord, are being transformed into the same image from one degree of glory to another. For this comes from the Lord who is the Spirit. (2 Corinthians 3:18)

My little children, I am writing these things to you so that you may not sin. But if anyone does sin, we have an advocate with the Father, Jesus Christ the righteous. (1 John 2:1)

Progress not Perfection

There will be victories and defeats in this Christian life, seasons of passion and pursuit of God, and seasons where it will feel like you are in a spiritual desert. God promises to preserve those who are truly found in him, and the journey is rarely a straight line of growth until we die.

God's standard is perfection.

You therefore must be perfect, as your heavenly Father is perfect. (Matthew 5:48)

But God also provides the one who is perfect to fulfill this requirement. As we grow, we grow in sanctification, and as we grow older, we should see progression.

Do we hate our sin more than we did yesterday, a week, a month ago? Do we love Christ more? We cannot usually objectively gauge this—just like a child does not feel themselves growing but their grandmother, after seeing them after several months exclaims "you are growing like a weed!" Perfection is clearly seen, just look at Jesus. Progress is sometimes less visible to us. We should ask others around us, "in what areas am I growing in—and in what areas do I need to grow?" Maturity is asking this question and responding to the answers in a non-defensive, open way.

Call Sin What It Is

We are called to holiness, purity and perfection (Matthew 5:48), but we know by our conduct that we cannot achieve that. Like the law showing us our sin, our inability to be perfect should humble us but not destroy us.

We will progress down a path, having victories on the way, but know that Satan does not want us to progress, our flesh cries out against us:

Be sober-minded; be watchful. Your adversary the devil prowls around like a roaring lion, seeking someone to devour. (1 Peter 5:8)

Wretched man that I am! Who will deliver me from this body of death? (Romans 7:24)

When we sin, let us call it exactly and specifically what it is, let us name our sin—Ray Ortlund, in his book <u>Death to Porn</u> emphasizes that we should not call our sin simply "stumbling" or "falling into sin." When we do this we confess to the general condition of feeling bad and knowing we have done wrong, and it lets us check the box of confession without feeling the true weight of how we have turned away from God and hurt other people.

When we look at pornography we do not "stumble"--we hurt our wives and tell her she is not worthy of our love, we hurt our future wives by bringing images to stain our minds and the purity of the marriage bed, we hurt our children and future children, we practice selfishness, we dishonor God and Christ's sacrifice on our behalf, we grieve the Holy Spirit, we don't believe that what God has for us is enough, we abuse and objectify the woman—those who are made in God's image, and so much more. We are a willing participant, we choose it, and we are culpable. God is completely just in condemning us because of our sin. When we sin, we should name it, feel the weight of it, confess it, repent of it.

If we confess our sins, he is faithful and just to forgive us our sins and to cleanse us from all unrighteousness. (1 John 1:9)

Let us not be light in letting ourselves off the hook—let us admit our sins, call them what they really are and run to the Father for forgiveness.

Only when we are honest about the nature of our sin can we truly repent of it—you cannot repent of "stumbling", because stumbling can happen by accident—and our sin is no accident. We cannot be called and held accountable by our brothers to change our behavior if we "stumble", but we can have true accountability and change if we confess sin and allow for correction and redirection to Christ's forgiveness. Let us cry out to God! Progress in the Christian life will be marked by addressing sin for what it is, remembering our gospel identity and and turning quickly to truth and worship.

Games

You are always playing a game, because consciously or subconsciously a pattern plays out in your life. When I am angry or feel annoyed, I pick on other people. I get a negative response. I act sullen and wounded. In the past, that woundedness would likely end up in turning inward, isolating and indulging in secret sexual sin. I have progressed, I am being sanctified, but when my unspoken or sinful expectations aren't met, it still results in sullenness and joylessness. By God's grace, this doesn't lead to indulging in secret sin anymore only because I confess earlier in the process. I know my game, I confess and repent faster with the knowledge that Satan is crouching at the door waiting to destroy me, my marriage, my family and my ministry.

What are your games? What do you turn to? What are the patterns that you see happen over and over? Are your patterns changing? Are you finding more joy over time or are you engaging in the self-sabotage of games? What sins are at the root of your games? The power of the Holy Spirit, Christ in us, disrupts the games–awareness leads to turning to the victory we have in Christ.

Root and Fruit

Once we have an awareness of the sin and we have confessed it, we must also begin digging to the root of the sin. Our sin is not simply the outward behavior, that is only the symptom of the manifestation of the sin we have in our hearts. Let us grow in awareness of the deep wickedness that flesh that still resides deep in the dark places of our hearts, let us ask the Father to burrow deep. It will be painful.

C.S. Lewis writes in the Voyage of the Dawn Treader about the ill-tempered Eustace who comes upon a dragon's lair with riches and *"Sleeping on a dragon's hoard with greedy, dragonish thoughts in his heart, he had become a dragon himself."* Eustace's transformation into a dragon had happened because of what was in his mind and heart. Later, Aslan the Lion, as the Christ figure, is the one that undoes the damage that Eustace has done and uses his claws to cut Eustace to the core, painfully stripping away his 'dragon's skin' of greed and bitterness towards the other characters and changing him back to being a boy. What's more, Eustace is thrown by Aslan into the water, cleansing him.

I hear echoes of Ezekiel 36 and John 3, and know that Lewis must have had the sprinkling of clean water to purify, and "you must be baptized of water and spirit" in those passages. I know what it is like to try to undo patterns of sin in my own life. It can't be done. It is Christ's work, and it is incredibly painful to shed your patterns and dragon-skin that you have built up over time because you don't even know you are a dragon. There must be cleansing of those sins, and repentance, and only Christ can strip away our old self and give us the purity that we need.

Go to the root. Go to the heart of your sin, only then can there be transformation. Whenever you sin, always ask yourself and begin to ask others "what is under, behind, what is at the foundation of the sin?" Confess to that deeper sin and give permission to your brothers to ask deeper questions—"What is behind that?--and how did you get there?" Gently restore your brothers and expect firm but gentle restoration!

Brothers if anyone is caught in any transgression, you who are spiritual should restore him in a spirit of gentleness. Keep watch on yourself, lest you too be tempted. (Galatians 6:1)

Specific Sin, Specific Truth, Specific Action and Identity

One way that we can overcome specific sin and lies are to overcome it with specific truth, as stated above, we must understand the root, then address with specificity the lie with the truth of the word along with action—what we do we sin tells us what we really want.

For example:

A man who runs to pornography has a comfort or control idol, in this situation they run to pornography when they feel insecure and unwanted.

The Specific Lie is that no one wants them, that their life has no value.

The Specific Truth to battle that lie: Christ has given them all things, Christ wants them—he is calling them, he bought them!

He who did not spare his own Son but gave him up for us all, how will he not also with him graciously give us all things? (Romans 8:32)

Come to me, all who labor and are heavy laden, and I will give you rest. (Matthew 11:28)

Flee from sexual immorality. Every other sin a person commits is outside the body, but the sexually immoral person sins against his own body. Or do you not know that your body is a temple of the Holy Spirit within you, whom you have from God? You are not your own, for you were bought with a price. So glorify God in your body. (1 Corinthians 6:18-20)

For to set the mind on the flesh is death, but to set the mind on the Spirit is life and peace. (Romans 8:6)

Oh! To have these truths stored up in our hearts as our identity! If every time we were alone in the dark, considering whether we would click an image or not, cross a line or not, and these verses came to our minds, so much more victory would be found in Christ and he would win the victory.

Specific Truth isn't just for a moment though, *Specific Truth* isn't just a panic button for a moment of sin—if I saw Romans 8:32, Matthew 11:28, 1 Corinthians 6:18-20, Romans 8:6 as my identity, I would be a man of action—every time I was confronted with the lie I would take action.

How did I get alone in the dark? How did the possibility of going to that website exist? Specific Truth leads to confession, repentance and ACTION—take a look at your guardrails, as we have journeyed and been accountable to one another in the last few weeks, do you need to adjust them? What sin patterns are still taking hold? How do you keep finding yourself in a compromising situation? Are you simply living from day to day reactively, or do you live proactively through your identity in Christ?

This is why scripture memorization is so important. Believers meditate on the truth of scripture so that it becomes our identity, not just a relief valve, a ejection seat or a balm when we feel shame–

Pastor Ben Stuart says:
"What you think about, you will care about, and what you care about, you will chase."

and I would add: "What you chase, you become."
What are you thinking about, what are you caring about, what are you chasing, what are you becoming?

O Victory in Jesus!

I often think (in a sinful and prideful way): "I am 40-something years old, I should have arrived by now" and that is a lie meant by the enemy to heap shame upon me.

There is no destination but Glory, our eternal home in heaven with Christ. You will not be totally free in this life from sin. You will still feel abandoned, forsaken, uncomfortable, insecure, and guilty. Instead of wallowing in our lack of victory, let us celebrate the victory we have in Christ! Satan would crush us in our wallowing, it is exactly what he wants:

For godly grief produces a repentance that leads to salvation without regret, whereas worldly grief produces death. (2 Corinthians 7:10)

When we sin, our first step should be a step towards Christ! Cry out to the one who can save us from ourselves.

Our feelings betray us, we feel guilty (and we are) and we want to absorb the penalty but cannot, it is too great and instant death and eternal suffering would be our consequence if we did.

Jesus' blood is effective to purify us, he knew our sin and yet chose to save us anyway. This is the objective reality for those who are found in him—the feeling "I am grieving in a worldly way because I have no hope" has one logical destination—suicide and death. We are Christians. We have hope.

Should we mourn our sin? Grieve it? Yes, but not long before we worship, dance for the victory we have over sin in Christ.

For thus says the One who is high and lifted up,
   who inhabits eternity, whose name is Holy:
"I dwell in the high and holy place,
   and also with him who is of a contrite and lowly spirit,
to revive the spirit of the lowly,
   and to revive the heart of the contrite. (Isaiah 57:15)

As I write this, another pastor I look up to has sinned and failed to live up to the biblical standard of an elder being above reproach—the world wants the spiritual leaders to fail, so that they can feel better about their own sin—this sin grabs the headlines. I don't know the end of this pastor's story, but as long as there is life, there is a chance for repentance, but the repentance will never make headlines—your repentance will never make headlines either, but it will affect generations of those you disciple and pour into.

Because you may never receive accolades for your repentance, it can seem like a lonely endeavor, but Christ's victory was also one that he did alone under the gaze of a loving Father—that same Father loves and pursues us—let us pursue him. Even for (and may be especially for) well known spiritual leaders, perfection will not be achieved, only Christ was perfect.

O Victory in Jesus,
My Savior, forever.
He sought me and bought me
With His redeeming blood;
He loved me ere I knew Him
And all my love is due Him,
He plunged me to victory,
Beneath the cleansing flood.
-O Victory in Jesus, Bartlett 1939

Don't Settle

Once we have had significant victory over sin, it is easy to look to the right and left and see those around you and say "with Christ's help, I have overcome much—time for me to stop pursuing holiness" and this, again, is an incredibly dangerous lie of Satan. Don't settle with the world's definition of holiness. Don't settle for your friends' or family's mediocre standard of holiness. Don't mistake Abide70's limited steps toward practicing good rhythms for holiness. There is more of Christ, there are deeper depths to plumb and higher heights to climb in him. There is more outward and inward sin to be killed, more flesh to be mortified. There is more to know of him, more to worship! Brothers, let us not settle, keep pressing on to know him more. This is how progress is made—we will be more and more like him until we die and then:

in a moment, in the twinkling of an eye, at the last trumpet. For the trumpet will sound, and the dead will be raised imperishable, and we shall be changed. (1 John 2:1)

Here in this life, it is progress not perfection, and if we persevere, it will be progress THEN- in heaven-perfection. We will be like our King, our Savior, our Advocate, our Friend, our Firstborn among many brothers, Jesus Christ.

Beloved, we are God's children now, and what we will be has not yet appeared; but we know that when he appears we shall be like him, because we shall see him as he is. (1 John 3:2)

Questions:

1. Do you feel like you should be further along by now? When you imagined yourself at the age you are now 5, 10, 20 years ago, do you think you would have arrived?

2. How do you describe your sin (I messed up, I stumbled, I fell again) Do you excuse yourself with your language? How might you change your language to reflect reality and your awareness of your sin?

3. Do you have a particular pattern of sin? What actions have you taken to get to the root of your sin? Have you explored wounds, abuses, neglects and patterns in your childhood that might make you more susceptible to certain types of sin? What idols are at the root of your sin (Control, Comfort)?

4. Are you settling for a standard of holiness and relationship with Christ that is lesser than his standard? Do you agree that you are influenced with your pursuit by how much others around you are pursuing? What can you do to break free of the world's (or your friends or the church's) standard of pursuing holiness?

5. Look at the paragraph, Specific Sin, Specific Truth, Specific Action and Identity: what is a real example of a sin you deal with that you need to address with a Specific Truth?

6. Have you given specific permission and coached brothers to ask the root questions-"What is behind that, what got you there?" Who will you give permission to do this? What Specific Action will you take against sin that continues to be habitual in your life?

7. What victories have you found in Christ's victory over sins in your life? Look back 5 and 10 years, are you more mature than you were then? Do you hate sin more? Do you love Christ more? In what ways? Celebrate the victory you have in Christ!

Session 7:
Abide in Christ's Humility

In Abide70, I hope you have experienced a failing of your will, a faltering of your resolve—you may have experienced being humbled. You've seen your lack. You've seen your need. The design of Abide70 is to emphasize your inability to grit your teeth and do everything you said you would do. You have failed. The longer we live our lives, the more we recognize that obedience is a daily battle, and we are always failing, and we only have Christ to hold on to. Ask for humility from the Father who gives good gifts. It takes boldness to pray for humility though, because what we are often praying for is humiliation, and in asking for it, the Lord often answers our prayers in ways we do not expect.

Humble like the Publican

He also told this parable to some who trusted in themselves that they were righteous, and treated others with contempt: "Two men went up into the temple to pray, one a Pharisee and the other a tax collector. The Pharisee, standing by himself, prayed thus: 'God, I thank you that I am not like other men, extortioners, unjust, adulterers, or even like this tax collector. I fast twice a week; I give tithes of all that I get.' But the tax collector, standing far off, would not even lift up his eyes to heaven, but beat his breast, saying, 'God, be merciful to me, a sinner!' I tell you, this man went down to his house justified, rather than the other. For everyone who exalts himself will be humbled, but the one who humbles himself will be exalted." (Luke 18:9-14)

As I have confessed, I am so prone to grumble, complain, and criticize. I am so prone to compare myself to others. I am so prone to dishonor God with my attitude of ungratefulness. Many times I am joyless and sullen. If I would recognize my true state, that I was a filthy sinner without merit or worth, I acknowledge my true state before God. I am not a better person because I get up early and read the Bible. I do not deserve a thumbs up, a pat on the back or kudos because I am more consistent at praying or a regular giver to Church or do family worship. I fail miserably even in the things that I try to be consistent in. If our devotion to Christ does not flow from our place of need, dependence on him, we are acting pridefully. Let us regularly fall at his feet and beg for his mercy and admit our dependence.

Humble Like John (the Baptist)

John answered them all, saying, "I baptize you with water, but he who is mightier than I is coming, the strap of whose sandals I am not worthy to untie. He will baptize you with the Holy Spirit and fire. (Luke 3:16)

Now a discussion arose between some of John's disciples and a Jew over purification. And they came to John and said to him, "Rabbi, he who was with you across the Jordan, to whom you bore witness—look, he is baptizing, and all are going to him." John answered, "A person cannot receive even one thing unless it is given him from heaven. You yourselves bear me witness, that I said, 'I am not the Christ, but I have been sent before him.' The one who has the bride is the bridegroom. The friend of the bridegroom, who stands and hears him, rejoices greatly at the bridegroom's voice.

Therefore this joy of mine is now complete. He must increase, but I must decrease. (John 3:25-30 emphasis added)

As new creations, a royal priesthood of believers in Christ, we have one purpose–

But you are a chosen race, a royal priesthood, a holy nation, a people for his own possession, that you may proclaim the excellencies of him who called you out of darkness into his marvelous light. (1 Peter 2:9)

John knew that he existed to point to, and continue to point to Jesus Christ. What if you saw this as your mission and your purpose? What if you reoriented the way you thought of your roles as a worker, a husband, a father, a brother, a friend? I am convinced that we are all John the Baptists, our entire lives terminating on a single point–that single point can only be darkness or light. John humbly made his single point the glory of Jesus Christ–begin thinking about your mission, what do you point to day in and day out? Your wealth? Your health? Your happiness and comfort? John got his wish of being decreased, diminished for the name of Christ–he (and all of the apostles) suffered greatly for his great Name. You must also decrease–he, Jesus Christ—must increase.

Humble Like Christ

Who has believed what he has heard from us?
*   And to whom has the arm of the Lord been revealed?*
For he grew up before him like a young plant,
*   and like a root out of dry ground;*

he had no form or majesty that we should look at him,
   and no beauty that we should desire him.
He was despised and rejected by men,
   a man of sorrows and acquainted with grief;
and as one from whom men hide their faces
   he was despised, and we esteemed him not.
Surely he has borne our griefs
   and carried our sorrows;
yet we esteemed him stricken,
   smitten by God, and afflicted.
But he was pierced for our transgressions;
   he was crushed for our iniquities;
upon him was the chastisement that brought us peace,
   and with his wounds we are healed.
All we like sheep have gone astray;
   we have turned—every one—to his own way;
and the Lord has laid on him
   the iniquity of us all.
He was oppressed, and he was afflicted,
   yet he opened not his mouth;
like a lamb that is led to the slaughter,
   and like a sheep that before its shearers is silent,
   so he opened not his mouth.
By oppression and judgment he was taken away;
   and as for his generation, who considered
that he was cut off out of the land of the living,
   stricken for the transgression of my people?
And they made his grave with the wicked
   and with a rich man in his death,
although he had done no violence,
   and there was no deceit in his mouth. (Isaiah 53:1-9)

Have this mind among yourselves, which is yours in Christ Jesus, who, though he was in the form of God, did not count equality with God a thing to be grasped, but emptied himself, by taking the form of a servant, being born in the likeness of men. And being found in human form, he humbled himself by becoming obedient to the point of death, even death on a cross (Philippians 2:5-8)

Jesus Christ was the only perfect man, the only one deserving of being able to gloat in triumph, to strut, to hold court of others, to complain and grumble about everyone around him, and yet, in every instance, he chose humility. How dare we demand that people honor our names? How could we grumble and complain when the perfect one, Jesus Christ who only was always continually sinned against did not? Oh! Let our mouths be stopped! Let us meditate on the perfect humility of Jesus and praise him, for if he had not humbled himself in our place, we would not receive the benefits of justification, sanctification, glorification!

How Do We Practice Humility?

First, see ourselves as people in need and we come to Jesus:

Take my yoke upon you, and learn from me, for I am gentle and lowly in heart, and you will find rest for your souls. (Matthew 11:29)

Jesus is giving us rest in his own humility—when he deserves to be wrathful towards us, he gently receives us in our sin and shame and shows us what true humility looks like. God delights to receive us in our suffering. We should have this same compassion for others, when we are wronged, we close our mouths. When we do not get the job, or the promotion or the relationship, or the return on the investment, or we are humiliated, we thank God for knowing and giving us exactly what we need.

Peter tells us:
Humble yourselves, therefore, under the mighty hand of God so that at the proper time he may exalt you, casting all your anxieties on him, because he cares for you. (1 Peter 5:6-7)

Our anxieties include all instances of where we do not believe we are getting what we bargained for, what we earned, what we deserve. God's hand is mighty, it is not a weak withholding hand, he has promised to give us all things (Romans 8:32) which certainly includes all things that we need, and that includes all suffering, all lack, all humiliation which causes us to grow closer to him. Peter follows this passage with this:

Be sober-minded; be watchful. Your adversary the devil prowls around like a roaring lion, seeking someone to devour (1 Peter 5:8)

When pride grows, when we feel like when have been wronged, we are standing on the precipice of a very dangerous cliff, we are naked and exposed in our own dependence on the flesh and look like a delicious piece of steak for the devil to devour—pride always precedes the fall.

Pride goes before destruction,

> *and a haughty spirit before a fall. (Proverbs 16:18)*

Ask the Lord for humility—but know that your prayer will likely be answered. John Newton, the author of the words to Amazing Grace, also wrote another well known hymn: "<u>I Asked the Lord that I Might Grow</u>" take time to listen to it—and pay close attention to the words.

The final lyrics are:

"Lord, why is this," I trembling cried,
"Wilt Thou pursue Thy worm to death?"
"'Tis in this way," the Lord replied,
"I answer prayer for grace and faith"

"These inward trials I employ
From self and pride to set thee free
And break thy schemes of earthly joy
That thou mayest seek thy all in Me."
(I Asked the Lord That I Might Grow, Newton, 1779)

Humble Yet Joyful

Humility is the path to joy—if you feel like you deserve nothing and have earned nothing, you will be overflowing with gratitude for what you have. If you are prideful, you will always be eyeing what you do not have. Paul rejoiced that Jesus granted him to suffer for the name of Jesus. What if we saw all dishonor, all shaming, all being passed over, all victory over sin and resisting temptation as favor? What if we saw all of it as a humbling so that we could be more like our Savior? Let us thank God for the suffering, for the humility, for the crushing.

And though the Lord give you the bread of adversity and the water of affliction, yet your Teacher will not hide himself anymore, but your eyes shall see your Teacher. And your ears shall hear a word behind you, saying, "This is the way, walk in it," when you turn to the right or when you turn to the left. (Isaiah 30:20-21)

It is God who humbles us, so that we might see him and listen to his voice, so our pride might die, and that we seek our all in the one who deserves all praise.

Questions:

1. Do you consider yourself a humble person? Rate your humility on a scale from 1-10, 10 being incredibly humble. Why would you rate yourself this way?

2. In what areas of your life do you find pride surfacing?

3. What permission do you need to give to others in your life to point out the sin of pride specifically? What do you need prayer for?

4. Do you pray regularly for humility? Why not?

5. In what ways has God humiliated you in order for you to see your pride and to humble you?

6. "Pride always to sin, and destruction"—in what ways has the Lord shown this to you? (Not a story about someone else, but you!)

7. Hallmarks of humility are:

   Meekness
   Simplicity (not practicing materialism)
   Gratefulness
   Contentedness
   Approachability
   Correctability
   Generosity, (Material)

Generosity, (Speech and Conduct)
Lowly
Serving
Going First (ways and places people don't want to go)
Going Last (when being first is of value)
Not Treating wife, kids, roommates as your servants
Not needing Control
Not needing Comfort

Rate yourself in each of these categories—allow the person closest to you to rate you as well (a close friend, your wife) pray for your heart in each of these categories and be ready to share with the Abide70 group where you want to grow.

Session 8:
Abide and Bear Much Fruit

I lift up my eyes to the hills. From where does my help come? My help comes from the Lord, who made heaven and earth. (Psalm 121:1-2)

Where there is no vision, the people perish (Proverbs 29:18a KJV)

I am the vine; you are the branches. Whoever abides in me and I in him, he it is that bears much fruit, for apart from me you can do nothing. (John 15:5)

Created to Bear Fruit

As we have journeyed together, we have confessed sin, challenged one another and asked for prayer and accountability—we know what we should be shedding:

Now the works of the flesh are evident: sexual immorality, impurity, sensuality, idolatry, sorcery, enmity, strife, jealousy, fits of anger, rivalries, dissensions, divisions, envy, drunkenness, orgies, and things like these. I warn you, as I warned you before, that those who do(such things will not inherit the kingdom of God. (Galatians 5:19-21)

But we know we are not to simply shed the works of the flesh and sit and wait for things to happen, when we are filled with the spirit, we have a new nature—God gives us the fruit of the Spirit.

But the fruit of the Spirit is love, joy, peace, patience, kindness, goodness, faithfulness, gentleness, self-control; against such things there is no law. And those who belong to Christ Jesus have crucified the flesh with its passions and desires. (Galatians 5:22-24)

We have a new nature, and we are now to position ourselves to serve others by the power of the Spirit–bearing fruit is the proof that we are in Christ.

So, every healthy tree bears good fruit, but the diseased tree bears bad fruit. A healthy tree cannot bear bad fruit, nor can a diseased tree bear good fruit. Every tree that does not bear good fruit is cut down and thrown into the fire. Thus you will recognize them by their fruits. (Matthew 7:17-20)

By this my Father is glorified, that you bear much fruit and so prove to be my disciples. (John 15:8)

The way that the fruit manifests is the way that we serve the body through our Spiritual gifts:

Now there are varieties of gifts, but the same Spirit; and there are varieties of service, but the same Lord; and there are varieties of activities, but it is the same God who empowers them all in everyone. To each is given the manifestation of the Spirit for the common good. For to one is given through the Spirit the utterance of wisdom, and to another the utterance of knowledge according to the same Spirit, to another faith by the same Spirit, to another gifts of healing by the one Spirit, to another the working of miracles, to another prophecy, to another the ability to distinguish between spirits, to another various kinds of tongues, to another the interpretation of tongues. All these are empowered by one and the same Spirit, who apportions to each one individually as he wills. (1 Corinthians 12:4-11)

We were given gifts, we use them to serve others for the common good the way that Christ served—we are to lay down our lives as a means of bearing fruit.

Truly, truly, I say to you, unless a grain of wheat falls into the earth and dies, it remains alone; but if it dies, it bears much fruit (John 12:24)

By this we know love, that he laid down his life for us, and we ought to lay down our lives for the brothers. (1 John 3:16)

We are called to die. We humble ourselves daily, dying daily to our own flesh, our desire to be served. If you are not currently serving the body, if you are not currently bearing much fruit, it may be that you are not dying to yourself. This has implications for the body—when one member of the body is lame or broken, it affects the whole, and your service to the whole is missed greatly.

Consider your mission and ministry: have you ever assessed what your gifts are, where you can plug in? Even in small ways, we can serve the body of Christ. Take some time to spend time with a church leader, your wife or a trusted brother in a discussion this week, asking them what they think your gifts are, where can you be used.

Vision

Most of us are in survival mode, working a job, paying bills, trying to keep the peace with the family, balancing busy schedules. This is merely surviving. As a man, you are given a role of authority and are uniquely positioned to provide leadership and vision. You do not have to follow the American culture as it blazes its trail to hell. Zoom out. Why are you here?

Do you believe that you and your family were created for something more?

Do you believe that you and your family were created for God's Glory?

Do you have a vision—God's vision of something more for you and your family?

If you do nothing, if you have no vision, you and your family and others in the body will perish—endeavor for something more—Joshua as the head of his people and family makes a case for the people of Israel to turn back to God:

"Now therefore fear the Lord and serve him in sincerity and in faithfulness. Put away the gods that your fathers served beyond the River and in Egypt, and serve the Lord. And if it is evil in your eyes to serve the Lord, choose this day whom you will serve, whether the gods your fathers served in the region beyond the River, or the gods of the Amorites in whose land you dwell. (Joshua 24:14-15a)

Joshua doesn't just give them the choice—he draws a line in the sand and casts a bold vision for his kin:

But as for me and my house, we will serve the Lord." (Joshua 25:15b)

Have you cast such a vision, and made such a bold statement for you and your family? Are you showing the distinction between serving our culture or serving Jesus? Do you regularly state and demonstrate your commitment to that vision? If you haven't to this point, you may feel timid or hypocritical to do such a thing—but today is a new day, and God's mercies are new. What would it look like for you to point yourself and your family in a direction that does not look like the world? You may have to confess your failure to do this in the past. Good. It will bring you more humility.

What would it look like to commit yourself to the high calling of Jesus, counting the cost and doing whatever it takes for your family not to fall into the clutches of the siren song of American culture's perverted sexual ethics, consumerism, materialism, humanism and secularism?

Mission

While vision is where we are going—mission is how we get there. In our culture, and even our subculture of the local church, it is easy to get caught up in a variety of different activities, but never really accomplish anything. Many of us know generally what are mission is supposed to be—

"Go therefore and make disciples of all nations, baptizing them in the name of the Father and of the Son and of the Holy Spirit," (Matthew 28:19)

We are commanded, but we don't have a real concept of how to execute. This can be daunting. If we aren't serving in a local context, we won't feel like we can talk to others about Jesus, because we have no connection to the greater body of Christ. If we don't have a direction or vision for our family, why would we call others to it? Finally, if we are so scattered, with no idea what it means to be "on mission" how in the world will we go, make disciples and baptize them?

We have been talking throughout these weeks about how helpful it is to have rhythms–hopefully they have been helpful–but what happens when Abide70 is over? Take time to prayerfully consider what the mission of your life is–and while the main point of it (spreading the Gospel) won't change–it may look different over the course of your life.

It is my challenge to you to put together your mission and share it with others, especially if you are married, share it with your wife, and if you have kids, share it with them: when we get distracted and decide to run after something new and shiny, having a mission statement holds you accountable what you have determined to be most important to the spiritual growth of you and your family and how you make decisions about your career and ministry in the body. When you do decide to do something different, when things in your life change, then you need to look at the mission and consider how it fits–and if it doesn't, you have a decision to make–you say "no" or you modify the mission (and perhaps eliminate something else) in order to accommodate the new opportunity.

In my personal experience, having a Mission Statement has been immensely helpful in pointing me towards what ministry (and other) opportunities I should pursue, and which ones I should wait on or say no to. Even good things can derail the overall mission.

I am sharing my Mission Statement as a part of Abide70. My hope is that it will be helpful as you think about how you can cast vision for your family, and create a plan to be "on mission." Your mission statement will not look like mine because the practicalities of each person's calling will be vastly different. However, as we've discussed, every believer's overall mission is "to glorify God and enjoy Him forever." Start there, and see how God is asking you to live it out through your calling, your mission!

"On Mission"

When my wife and I have the least conflict, when I deal with the least besetting sin, when I feel the least temptation, when I feel the most joy and worship is when I am "on mission." It is a code and short conversation with my wife, really helpful right before I go into a stressful situation where I could lose my head (like a family holiday gathering or an interaction with someone I am in conflict with):
"On mission?"
"Check. On mission"
If you have never felt this "on mission-ness", it is probably because you are where I have been, and often am: just going

with the flow, swimming with the stream of worldliness, reactively waiting on things to happen rather than living out God's mission, and the values reflected in my Mission Statement. When I am worried about "my"self, "my" money, "my" future, "my" comfort, "my" control, I am not on a mission.

O! That we would turn our eyes upon Jesus, that we would see that we are God's people, and truly believe it, we would proclaim in word and deed Christ's glory! We would be "fishers of men" walking in our true purpose and be "on mission!"

A Note About Vocation/Location vs. Mission

What we do for a job is not who we truly are–and yet this is the way that we define ourselves to the world. You are not your job–it is only a role you fulfill. Your identity is in Christ. Your job is simply the workplace that God sovereignly put you in to fulfill the mission of "proclaiming his excellencies!". Do you think of your job this way?

Think about the chain of events that it took for God to literally move heaven and earth in order to place you in your neighborhood and have the neighbors that you do–it isn't an accident, he is sovereign! You are the missionary he has given to your co-workers and neighbors. Proclaim his excellencies with boldness. If you are married, you have been uniquely positioned to proclaim his excellencies through the way you lead and love, and if you have kids, how you shepherd them in this mission.

Sola Scriptura, Soli Deo Gloria!

It would be easy to write your Mission Statement to aim for worldly pursuits, that it simply would be an exercise in making goals to further your glory. In your casting vision and creating mission, look to scripture to give you a guide, to show you the truth–hold these documents up to scripture to see if they line up with God's glory–or yours.

Oh, the depth of the riches and wisdom and knowledge of God! How unsearchable are his judgments and how inscrutable his ways!

"For who has known the mind of the Lord,

or who has been his counselor?"

"Or who has given a gift to him

that he might be repaid?"

For from him and through him and to him are all things. To him be glory forever. Amen. (Romans 11:33-36)

Questions: (There is more homework associated with this session, plan accordingly, see resources appendix for sample mission statement)

1. Do you feel like you are currently bearing fruit? What is the evidence?

2. Have you assessed your gifts? Ask your spouse or brother what your gifts are—are you using them in a ministry context?

3. Have you cast Vision for yourself, for your family recently? What is your plan for casting vision for yourself and family? What stops you from sharing this with your family?

4. Create a mission statement, be prepared to share it with the group and receive feedback. (See appendix for sample mission statement)

*Note: The next sessions have 'Married' and 'Unmarried' versions—pick the one that describes you.

Session 9 (Married): Christ Pursued

We love because he first loved us. (1 John 4:19.)

Blessed be the God and Father of our Lord Jesus Christ, who has blessed us in Christ with every spiritual blessing in the heavenly places, even as he chose us in him before the foundation of the world, that we should be holy and blameless before him. In love he predestined us for adoption to himself as sons through Jesus Christ, according to the purpose of his will, to the praise of his glorious grace, with which he has blessed us in the Beloved. (Ephesians 1:3-6)

I have been crucified with Christ. It is no longer I who live, but Christ who lives in me. And the life I now live in the flesh I live by faith in the Son of God, who loved me and gave himself for me. (Galatians 2:20)

He who did not spare his own Son but gave him up for us all, how will he not also with him graciously give us all things? (Romans 8:32)

Christ As Pursuer

Recently we covered humility: and the first thing in your humility you need to know is this: you were not smart enough, good enough, or born in the right place in order to come to God–Jesus chose you with his choosing love before the foundation of the earth, he pursued you in your rebellion against him and called you to himself, reconciling us to God.

Therefore, if anyone is in Christ, he is a new creation. The old has passed away; behold, the new has come. All this is from God, who through Christ reconciled us to himself and gave us the ministry of reconciliation; that is, in Christ God was reconciling the world to himself, not counting their trespasses against them, and entrusting to us the message of reconciliation. (2 Corinthians 5:17-19)

Christ pursued you, and maybe it was your mom, a youth pastor, a friend, but they spoke the gospel to you and you believed and became Christ's! Aside from Christ, what believer was it who pursued you?

And once you have answered that question the new question becomes, "who are you pursuing?"

Pursue God

All of Abide70 has been about meeting with God and pursuing him, making him the object of our everlasting joy–

Let us know; let us press on to know the Lord;
  his going out is sure as the dawn;
he will come to us as the showers,
  as the spring rains that water the earth." (Hosea 6:3)

Not that I have already obtained this or am already perfect, but I press on to make it my own, because Christ Jesus has made me his own. Brothers, I do not consider that I have made it my own. But one thing I do: forgetting what lies behind and straining forward to what lies ahead, I press on toward the goal for the prize of the upward call of God in Christ Jesus. (Philippians 3:12-14)

We pursue, we press on. When Abide70 ends in a few days do not stop pursuing, do not stop pressing on!

Pursue your Wife

This topic could fill an entire 70 days of focus—As a married man, it is your role to pursue the heart of your wife, to lead her to Jesus. This is no easy task, and I know that I am the foremost in failing at this.

Your goal isn't to make your wife happy in you, you press on to make her happy in Jesus Christ. You do not nag or mansplain her into having a relationship with God. You do not belittle or berate her, you don't coerce or manipulate. Know her. Consider her. Live with her in an understanding way:

Likewise, husbands, live with your wives in an understanding way, showing honor to the woman as the weaker vessel, since they are heirs with you of the grace of life, so that your prayers may not be hindered. (1 Peter 3:7)

Many have trouble with this verse, especially if we have wives who seem to outshine us in holiness and toughness—we see ourselves as the weaker vessel. The 'weaker vessel' does not imply any derogatory meaning here, but speaks to how valuable and precious our wives are—like a delicate and priceless vase, if we handle her without care, we can abuse the gentleness and kindness that is found in our wife. We are to nurture her and not take her for granted. There are high stakes here—we are to treat her with kindness and gentleness and not carelessly and roughly—or our prayers will be hindered—God refuses to listen to the requests of a man that abuses the kindness of his wife!

Strive to love her like Jesus loves the Church—

Husbands, love your wives, as Christ loved the church and gave himself up for her, that he might sanctify her, having cleansed her by the washing of water with the word, so that he might present the church to himself in splendor, without spot or wrinkle or any such thing, that she might be holy and without blemish. In the same way, husbands should love their wives as their own bodies. He who loves his wife loves himself. For no one ever hated his own flesh, but nourishes and cherishes it, just as Christ does the church, because we are members of his body. "Therefore a man shall leave his father and mother and hold fast to his wife, and the two shall become one flesh. (Ephesians 5:25-30)

This is a convicting and high calling—read it over and over, and make application for how you will apply this in your mission statement that you wrote last week, maybe it needs to be modified to incorporate how you will nurture and cherish your wife, how you will date her, show her how valuable she is and wash her in the water of the word. As married men, we all fail to show our wives kindness and gratefulness—these things should flow from our thankfulness to God in his sovereign choosing of our wife.

Enjoy life with the wife whom you love, all the days of your vain life that he has given you under the sun, because that is your portion in life and in your toil at which you toil under the sun. (Ecclesiastes 9:9)

Do you find yourself enjoying life with your wife? Some days and seasons it feels painful and full of drudgery—the mundanity of working, paying bills, family dynamics and parenting can disconnect us from the thrill and intimacy that we once knew, and it can be tempting to chase that somewhere else—a co-worker, an old girlfriend, an image on the computer screen, etc. We are lazy and want easy intimacy—but this leads to death.

If you find yourself in a difficult season of marriage, press into the pain, begin again to cultivate the intimacy you once pursued with your wife. First, lead her in worship and prayer—apologize to her for neglecting this aspect, and establish a regular time to pray over her (with her) and for her (alone). Truly desire for her to grow. Coercing and pushing won't change her heart, but prayer promises to.

Put your money where your mouth is—begin being attentive to her again, this doesn't have to be expensive. Finding childcare and going away for a short weekend or even just going for a walk, make her a priority, no distractions. A date night doesn't solve all your problems, cultivate regular times of intentional, no-strings attached time with her. Ask her how you are doing as a husband, spiritually, financially, around the house, in the area of physical intimacy. Ask her what you could do better and be ready to be humbled, don't make excuses, or even give "reasons." Listen and be approachable.

Front Burner

My wife and I have developed some good habits and routines over the years, and one recent development is the idea of the "Front Burner" issue: what is the one thing that your wife needs you to do (and she may be telling it to you all the time) but that you neglect because it is low on your priority list? This is the thing that festers in her mind and grows distance and bitterness between you—maybe you have a "front burner" item too—ask your wife what is her "front burner" issue—what is the highest priority thing that only you can take care of or can help her accomplish? It may be something small like putting your keys in the key basket—it may be something bigger like a purchase of a new dryer because the clothes aren't getting dry, it may be something to do with your physical intimacy—but there may be one thing that you will have to swallow your pride and do, buy or do differently, simply because it is a high priority for your wife and you need to consider her needs higher than yours (Philippians 2:3)

Physical Intimacy

Let your fountain be blessed,
  and rejoice in the wife of your youth,
  a lovely deer, a graceful doe.
Let her breasts fill you at all times with delight;
  be intoxicated always in her love. (Proverbs 5:18-19)

The intimacy between a husband and wife can be one of the biggest sources of joy and frustration in any marriage.

But because of the temptation to sexual immorality, each man should have his own wife and each woman her own husband. The husband should give to his wife her conjugal rights, and likewise the wife to her husband. For the wife does not have authority over her own body, but the husband does. Likewise the husband does not have authority over his own body, but the wife does. Do not deprive one another, except perhaps by agreement for a limited time, that you may devote yourselves to prayer; but then come together again, so that Satan may not tempt you because of your lack of self-control. (1 Corinthians 7:2-5)

How are you pursuing your wife in this way—and in what ways are you being selfish in this area? I can't be expansive in my comments in this format, I will simply give this advice: If you are not having regular conversations about expectations that are gentle, kind and patient on the topic of sexual intimacy, both of of you will likely be frustrated: consider your wife, learn what brings her pleasure, and seek to serve her in this area.

You will experience different seasons as you learn to navigate intimacy with your wife, and if you have been married longer than 3 months, you probably already know this. Have older, Bible-minded brothers who can encourage you and correct you in your thinking in this area—don't complain or be crude or crass, seek to grow in knowledge in the area of pleasing your wife—you don't get this from the world, but seek wisdom in the Bible and by simply asking your wife questions about her expectations.

There are many instances when healing for past sins, abuse, and wrong-thinking must be addressed in these conversations—there is no quick solution, seek godly counsel when approaching this topic and be gentle and patient.

Encourage your wife to have relationships with older, godly women who have been married longer who are willing to have frank and open discussions about sexual intimacy.

Older women likewise are to be reverent in behavior, not slanderers or slaves to much wine. They are to teach what is good, and so train the young women to love their husbands and children, to be self-controlled, pure, working at home, kind, and submissive to their own husbands, that the word of God may not be reviled. (Titus 2:3-5)

You will have to give permission for such conversations to take place and swallow your pride. Is your wife in a relationship with an older woman who will walk with her in this area?

Lust, Pornography, Affairs, Etc.

We have already addressed sexual sin on many levels during Abide70, but it needs to be said that marriage is to reflect the purity of Christ—we are to keep the marriage bed pure and undefiled—bringing envy, lust, pornography, masturbation, fantasies, flirting and affairs into the marriage bed will bring conflict and death to your marriage. None of us are immune to any of this:

Be sober-minded; be watchful. Your adversary the devil prowls around like a roaring lion, seeking someone to devour. (1 Peter 5:8)

Put up guardrails, eliminate images, too-familiar relationships with women not your wife, stumbling blocks, and be on guard—go back to your mission, go back to the early weeks of Abide70 and evaluate what you will make permanent to protect your eyes and your heart—Satan means for lust, pornography, masturbation, fantasies, flirting and affairs (physical or emotional) to bring death to your marriage. If you have sinned in these ways, confess and repent, the blood of Christ covers you. Seek reconciliation with your wife, get in community with other men who will hold you accountable, and seek marriage counsel from older and biblically wiser couples.

Marriage is Temporary, God's Glory is Forever

For in the resurrection they neither marry nor are given in marriage, but are like angels in heaven. (Matthew 22:30)

Even though we won't be married in heaven, God is sovereign, and he created you before the foundation of the world to be the husband of the wife you have in the here and now—the suffering that you experience in marriage through and alongside your wife is preparing you for the eternal weight of Glory (2 Corinthians 4:17)—and one day, Lord willing, you will rejoice in heaven as brother and sister in

God's heavenly kingdom, rejoicing in a way that is deeper than the deepest joys we can experience in our earthly marriage, more pleasurable than the heights of pleasure that we experienced together in the intimacy of our earthly marriage! God's glory is forever!

The image of a husband and wife living as one flesh is the image of Christ and the Church—we can never measure up to Christ, the bridegroom—but while we have breath in us, let us endeavor to pursue and love our wives as Christ loves the church!

Pursue Your Children

If you have kids, after your wife, this is your number one mission—it comes above your job, above your ministry, and if you fail here, you aren't qualified for ministry.

if anyone is above reproach, the husband of one wife, and his children are believers and not open to the charge of debauchery or insubordination. For an overseer, as God's steward, must be above reproach. (1 Timothy 5:6-7)

There are so many admonitions in scripture to train your children, to raise them with gentleness and not harshness. Disciple them—point to Christ. They don't need opportunity, or a good education so they can get good jobs and have successful lives, what they need is the healing and forgiveness of Jesus Christ. You cannot make them believers, but you can "put the kindling" around them from the time they are very small, loving and leading them well.

If you cannot disciple your own kids, how will you disciple other men? If you have failed here, again, what is needed is reorientation: confess, cast vision, and start pursuing them!

Give them the Gospel

There is both an illustration and truth in this passage:
"Ask, and it will be given to you; seek, and you will find; knock, and it will be opened to you. For everyone who asks receives, and the one who seeks finds, and to the one who knocks it will be opened. Or which one of you, if his son asks him for bread, will give him a stone? Or if he asks for a fish, will give him a serpent? If you then, who are evil, know how to give good gifts to your children, how much more will your Father who is in heaven give good things to those who ask him! (Matthew 7:7-11)

First, we're evil, but we still know instinctively what our children need, even if we sometimes withhold it from them. Second, God is the Father we are to emulate, and we will never measure up…but third, in our not measuring up, we can ask our perfect and good Father for the ability to be better dads, despite our own checkered heritages, we can, by God's power, leave gospel legacies for our children.

Pursue them by Proclaiming the Gospel to Them

"Hear, O Israel: The Lord our God, the Lord is one. You shall love the Lord your God with all your heart and with all your soul and with all your might. And these words that I command you today shall be on your heart. You shall teach them diligently to your children, and shall talk of them when you sit

in your house, and when you walk by the way, and when you lie down, and when you rise. You shall bind them as a sign on your hand, and they shall be as frontlets between your eyes. You shall write them on the doorposts of your house and on your gates. (Deuteronomy 6:4-9)

But as for you, continue in what you have learned and have firmly believed, knowing from whom you learned it and how from childhood you have been acquainted with the sacred writings, which are able to make you wise for salvation through faith in Christ Jesus. (1 Timothy 3:4-5)

Like you, your kids need the Gospel every day, just like you, they need to abide in the power of Christ! Put in place a practice of daily worship–it doesn't have to be complex–you are now reading the Word every day–tell them what you are reading, or read a parable to them, tie it to the truth of the Gospel and sing a song, then pray–even if they are very young and can't hold still for 2 minutes, these 2 minutes are the most important of the day. Let them grow up never remembering a time without family worship–and if your kids are older, confess and apologize to them, humble yourself and tell them: "our family worships God–this is something we are committed to daily!"

Pursue them By Disciplining them

This is a controversial topic, so I will draw largely upon scripture and not my opinions in this area: first, we can all agree that biblically, we are commanded to discipline our children:

Fathers, do not provoke your children to anger, but bring them up in the discipline and instruction of the Lord. (Ephesians 6:4)

This verse comes with instructions for us: we are not to provoke, we are not to be harsh, we are not to set our expectations too high, we are to be humble. We are also to discipline them in the Lord and instruct them in the Lord. This is what we are required to do as dads.

A Theology of Discipline

And have you forgotten the exhortation that addresses you as sons?
"My son, do not regard lightly the discipline of the Lord,
 nor be weary when reproved by him.
For the Lord disciplines the one he loves,
 and chastises every son whom he receives."
It is for discipline that you have to endure. God is treating you as sons. For what son is there whom his father does not discipline? If you are left without discipline, in which all have participated, then you are illegitimate children and not sons. Besides this, we have had earthly fathers who disciplined us and we respected them. Shall we not much more be subject to the Father of spirits and live? For they disciplined us for a short time as it seemed best to them, but he disciplines us for our good, that we may share his holiness. For the moment all discipline seems painful rather than pleasant, but later it yields the peaceful fruit of righteousness to those who have been trained by it. (Hebrews 12:5-17, emphasis added)

How do we know that we are sons? Because we received the discipline of the Lord—if we do not practice regular, kind, non-anger based, gospel-centered discipline in our houses, then how will our children understand the discipline of the Lord?

Discipline will look different in every household, and will even vary from child to child, but there are a couple of principles we need to agree on:

Children, like everyone, are sinful

Therefore, just as through one man sin entered into the world, and death through sin, and so death spread to all men, because all sinned—(Romans 5:12)

for all have sinned and fall short of the glory of God, (Romans 3:23)

Your precious 10-month old is sinful—they are testing limits, seeing if your "no" means "no". When you lack consistency in your discipline, you are reinforcing sin!

Your smart-mouthed 17-year old is sinful—they are testing limits, seeing if your "no" means "no". When you lack consistency in your discipline, you are reinforcing sin!

Discipline is usually physical, especially early in life:

Do not withhold discipline from a child; if you strike him with a rod, he will not die. If you strike him with the rod, you will save his soul from hell. (Proverbs 23:13-14)

Whoever spares the rod hates his son, but he who loves him is diligent to discipline him. (Proverbs 13:24)

This is strong language–physical discipline is closely connected with saving your child's soul from hell and with your love for him. While many disagree with physical discipline, it is because they have seen it done poorly or because the world tells them it is wrong, and it is true that it is often done sinfully and in anger. <u>Physical discipline done in anger IS sin.</u> I have committed this sin, and if you have, you need to confess, ask forgiveness from God and your children and your spouse, and repent. The scriptural admonition to discipline your children in a way that is physical isn't just a cultural norm of a bygone era. To think that we have "moved past this and we are more civilized now" is chronological snobbery. There must be a category for physical discipline that is Gospel-based.

A Framework for Christ-centered Physical Discipline

Below is a framework for Christ-centered discipline that has been beneficial in my house:

1. As soon as a child can disobey you, they are ready for physical discipline:

    I remember the first time I saw true disobedience in my first child: As my 10 month-old reached for a cabinet door I had distracted him and moved him away from several times, I told him "no, no" in a deep voice which was our way of telling him that something was hands off. He looked at me as he slowly reached for the door—he knew that he shouldn't, and yet he was testing me, seeing what would happen next. It was at that opportunity, we first introduced a light slap on the hand as a connect between physical pain and disobedience—if you start early, they learn very quickly. Your child should never be able allowed to disobey or to tell you no, unless you've given them an option. So be mindful of commands and establish the authority they're crying out for. Your authority is their direct connection to God's authority. Teach them how to disobey you, and you're teaching them how to disobey their Creator.

2. Consistency:

    If you haven't been until now—know that consistency is key. You have to bring the consequences to your children EVERY SINGLE TIME: if sometimes they can get away with disobeying, and other times they can't, you are creating an unstable environment—you are introducing an element of chaos into their life and they are finding that they cannot rely on your consistency, that they can take a gamble with disobedience, because sometimes they can get away with it. They'll learn how to push your boundaries and manipulate you. They must know that you say what you mean, or they will take advantage (remember, they are sinful!). Don't make an ultimatum if you aren't willing to follow through.

3. Give Them the Gospel Again and Again.

They won't understand this at first, and they have a short attention span, so keep it brief early on. As they get older, there is a gospel conversation that needs to happen with every time they receive physical discipline: I have not used the word punishment in this topic so far, because <u>discipline is not punishment</u>. If we are in Christ, we do not receive punishment for our sin, and if your child professes to love Jesus as many children of christian parents do, they are not ever going to receive the punishment for their sins if they are chosen in him, so we need to stop using that language. Christ took the punishment for all of our sins, so we must be careful not to associate punishment with spankings. Our theology must match the way that we discipline—at my house the conversation goes like this:

Me: Do you need a spanking?
Child: Yes.
Me: Why do you need a spanking?
Child: Because...(reason)
Me: Why do we discipline— is it because you are being punished?
Child: Uh…? (Blank stare)
Me: No, because Christ took all your punishment at the cross—God is full of grace and mercy for you, let's pursue Christ together! The reason you are getting a spanking is that sin ALWAYS has consequences, even if we don't see them right away— (often I will confess my own sin and where I have seen consequences at this point) just because you aren't taking punishment does not mean there aren't consequences for sin. (For older children who can understand, this is also a good

time to talk about God loving us through discipline. It's how he keeps us in Christ! You've been on this journey of disciplining your own mind and body for the purpose of abiding in Christ…pass this on to your child!)

Then I spank them, then we hug, cry together and often pray. Be vulnerable, speak of the times that you have seen consequences of your sin, and the painful "spankings" you have experienced and how it turned you back to God. I explain to them that just like if you walked out in the street, you could get hit by a car—there are consequences, and we are trying to connect the consequence to sinful disobedience. You will spank your children 100, 500, 1000, 10,000 times—every single time is an opportunity for gospel and reconciliation. Don't miss the opportunity. Don't punish your children. It isn't your job. Spanking should be done in a controlled environment, behind a closed door (not for public shaming), it should be close in time to the disobedience unless you are angry.

4. Your Sinful Anger.

If you are angry, you must distance yourself from it. Never physically discipline in anger, you need to internalize the same Gospel that you are delivering to your children, and practice self-control. When your children are disobedient to your wife, encourage her to send your kids to you so that you can spank in objective love for your children, and allow emotional distance for her. You are much stronger than your children and that can be abused. Physical discipline shouldn't take the form of bullying, grabbing, yanking, shaking or shaming your children—it should always be done, pleading them to turn to Jesus and his forgiveness for them! Tell them verses about running to Jesus, we have made liberal use of Matthew 11:28 in this study!

Pursuing your kids in this way is not provoking them. In their disobedience, drive them to the grace and forgiveness of Christ!

If you believe that children should never be disciplined in this way, I encourage you to wrestle with the scriptural passages that deal with discipline. And the dire consequences that result when we do not discipline them well.

Special Circumstances

There are special circumstances for children who have been victims of abuse or children who are in your foster care or adopted: use wisdom and follow guidelines that authorities have put in place.

Pursue other Men

It's time.

And Jesus went throughout all the cities and villages, teaching in their synagogues and proclaiming the gospel of the kingdom and healing every disease and every affliction. When he saw the crowds, he had compassion for them, because they were harassed and helpless, like sheep without a shepherd. Then he said to his disciples, "The harvest is plentiful, but the laborers are few; therefore pray earnestly to the Lord of the harvest to send out laborers into his harvest." (Matthew 9:35-38)

You are the laborers. If you have gone through Abide70 this far, you have to come to the realization that pointing outward, being on mission is the goal of what God has for us. Look around, who is in your sphere of influence? Who do you work with? Who are your unbelieving family members? Who do you workout with? Where do you like to recreate? Pursue. Pursue. Pursue these men, form a new group, go through Abide70 with them, point them to the truth. If you think you aren't ready, it is just an excuse. It is in the doing that you become ready.

Name Them and Pursue Them

Make a list of the different places where you have influence: write down the names of the men who you will begin pursuing: it may only be 1 or 2 at first, and there will be much failure and disappointment–do not become hardened: like our Lord, have compassion on the lost–pray for them! You have a high calling:

Therefore, we are ambassadors for Christ, God making his appeal through us. We implore you on behalf of Christ, be reconciled to God. (2 Corinthians 5:20)

Let us pursue, let us seek those who are lost, those who need to grow, and invite them to the feast!

Questions:

1. Do you feel like you are pursuing the heart of your wife for Christ well? Why or why not?

2. Do you have mature men you can speak to and ask questions about marital physical intimacy to get Biblical wisdom (without resorting to boasting, dishonoring your wife, lewdness, locker room talk or crassness?)

3. If you are a parent, do you feel like you are pursuing your children's hearts for Christ? What are you doing? What is the evidence? What are your thoughts on corporal discipline?

4. Do you feel equipped to lead your own Abide70 or a Bible study, or other curriculum with a group of guys? What stops you from pursuing men like this?

5. Who are the guys you will be pursuing? What are you doing to pursue them, how can we pray for them by name?

Session 9 (Unmarried):
Christ Pursued

We love because he first loved us. (1 John 4:19.)

Blessed be the God and Father of our Lord Jesus Christ, who has blessed us in Christ with every spiritual blessing in the heavenly places, even as he chose us in him before the foundation of the world, that we should be holy and blameless before him. In love he predestined us for adoption to himself as sons through Jesus Christ, according to the purpose of his will, to the praise of his glorious grace, with which he has blessed us in the Beloved. (Ephesians 1:3-6)

I have been crucified with Christ. It is no longer I who live, but Christ who lives in me. And the life I now live in the flesh I live by faith in the Son of God, who loved me and gave himself for me. (Galatians 2:20)

He who did not spare his own Son but gave him up for us all, how will he not also with him graciously give us all things? (Romans 8:32)

Christ As Pursuer

Last week, we covered humility: and the first thing in your humility you need to know is this: you were not smart enough, good enough, or born in the right place in order to come to God—Jesus chose you with his choosing love before the foundation of the earth, he pursued you in your rebellion against him and called you to himself, reconciling us to God.

Therefore, if anyone is in Christ, he is a new creation. The old has passed away; behold, the new has come. All this is from God, who through Christ reconciled us to himself and gave us the ministry of reconciliation; that is, in Christ God was reconciling the world to himself, not counting their trespasses against them, and entrusting to us the message of reconciliation. (2 Corinthians 5:17-19)

Christ pursued you, and maybe it was your mom, a youth pastor, a friend, but they spoke the gospel to you and you believed and became Christ's! Aside from Christ, what believer was it who pursued you?

And once you have answered that question the new question becomes, "who are you pursuing?"

Pursue God

All of Abide70 has been about meeting with God and pursuing him, making him the object of our everlasting joy–

Let us know; let us press on to know the Lord;
 his going out is sure as the dawn;
he will come to us as the showers,
 as the spring rains that water the earth." (Hosea 6:3)

Not that I have already obtained this or am already perfect, but I press on to make it my own, because Christ Jesus has made me his own. Brothers, I do not consider that I have made it my own. But one thing I do: forgetting what lies behind and straining forward to what lies ahead, I press on toward the goal for the prize of the upward call of God in Christ Jesus. (Philippians 3:12-14)

We pursue, we press on! When Abide70 ends in a few days do not stop pursuing, do not stop pressing on.

Pursue A Wife

If you are not married, there are applications to be made for pursuing a wife:

*He who finds a wife finds a good thing
    and obtains favor from the Lord. (Proverbs 18:22)*

If you are single, and have no desire to pursue a wife—there is provision for this:

First, Christ was single—he had no divided interest—his whole purpose was to fulfill the will of his Father. We know that Paul was single, he either was unmarried or a widower:

"To the unmarried and the widows I say that it is good for them to remain single, as I am." (1 Corinthians 7:8)

I want you to be free from anxieties. The unmarried man is anxious about the things of the Lord, how to please the Lord. But the married man is anxious about worldly things, how to please his wife, and his interests are divided. (1 Corinthians 7:32-34a)

So then he who marries his betrothed does well, and he who refrains from marriage will do even better. (1 Corinthians 7:38)

Paul thinks you are better off unmarried—but with a condition: the unmarried man is anxious for, zealous for, pursuing with passion the things of the Lord. The unmarried man is not unmarried because he simply "can't find a wife" or is "dating around" he is unmarried because he has undivided interests, his passion is to be unmarried so that he can serve the body of Christ with all his power—giving up the joy and pleasures of sex in marriage, companionship and children, sacrificing these desires in exclusive service to God and his Church. Singleness in our American culture means having options, being free from responsibility, and a free sexual ethic, be careful that if you have chosen singleness, it is rooted in scripture, not the world's idea of singleness.

To the unmarried and the widows I say that it is good for them to remain single, as I am. But if they cannot exercise self-control, they should marry. For it is better to marry than to burn with passion. (1 Corinthians 7:8-9)

Paul is not giving provision for sin here (if they cannot exercise self-control...) see Romans 6:1. What Paul is giving provision and permission for is the ability to take natural sexual passion and devote it wholly to one woman for your entire life—if you are a single man you should either be:

1. Self-controlled, not burning with passion, celibate (including lust, masturbation and pornography)and seeking Christ with all your power, no intention of getting married
   or–

2. Self-controlled, celibate (including lust, masturbation and pornography) and seeking Christ with the intention of getting married, pursuing a wife.

There really is no third category—A couple words of advice for men who are in category 2:

- Pursue Christ: it is in the pursuit of Christ and making him your joy, that you will become more like him. Women who also want to pursue Christ will come alongside, and that is the woman you want—if she does not love Christ, you will not "save her" into it!
- Pursue purity: Every woman you look at lustfully, every time you use pornography, have sex with someone not your wife, practice masturbation and pursue images, that becomes a part of who you are—you are defiling the marriage bed even before marriage—you are changed in your expectations for sexual intimacy—seek purity, first for joyful obedience to Christ, but also so that you might fully delight in your wife!
- Become the man of honor before you pursue her: How do you find a wife? Besides the first two points here, one is to become the man who would attract the kind of wife you are looking for. If you are addicted to video games and pornography, you can't get up on time, you are lazy and messy, unprincipled, can't provide financially for, don't disciple others and don't speak truth, how will you find a wife who values these things? You don't become these things after you are married—you are the man today who your wife will

marry—and if you aren't the man today that you aspire to be, then endeavor to change!
- Pursue Biblical community: This is quite simple. Where do Godly women go? Become part of the church community where there are Godly single men and women. Don't make excuses about being introverted or having work priorities or not knowing what to do. Don't neglect community. People usually make Church something that they can fit in if possible, and it is the first thing to get cut out if something comes up. Make the Church community a priority of your life, it is not a guarantee you will meet your future wife, but we are commanded to meet together and to serve together.
- Serve the Body: Serve the body of Christ joyfully. Often, in serving you will meet others with similar interests, and marriage is about serving the body together. In serving, a Godly woman will often find a man and a man, a woman who is already doing what they are supposed to be doing. Be "on mission"!
- Be patient....: God sees you and knows your situation—he knows what he has for you—don't let the passage of time give you an excuse to pursue sin. Even if you never find a wife, becoming a man after God's own heart will be worth the obedience and effort and all of the suffering and joy you will experience in the waiting.
- DO SOMETHING: Pursue! A Godly woman won't just find you, pursue you and ask you to marry her—that is not how this works. You are a man—it is your role to step out in boldness. Examine your standards—do

you even know what you are looking for in a wife? Take some time to read Proverbs 31:

An excellent wife who can find?
She is far more precious than jewels.
The heart of her husband trusts in her,
and he will have no lack of gain.
She does him good, and not harm,
all the days of her life.
She seeks wool and flax,
and works with willing hands.
She is like the ships of the merchant;
she brings her food from afar.
She rises while it is yet night
and provides food for her household
and portions for her maidens.
She considers a field and buys it;
with the fruit of her hands she plants a vineyard.
She dresses herself with strength
and makes her arms strong.
She perceives that her merchandise is profitable.
Her lamp does not go out at night.
She puts her hands to the distaff,
and her hands hold the spindle.
She opens her hand to the poor
and reaches out her hands to the needy.
She is not afraid of snow for her household,
for all her household are clothed in scarlet.
She makes bed coverings for herself;
her clothing is fine linen and purple.
Her husband is known in the gates
when he sits among the elders of the land.

> *She makes linen garments and sells them;*
> *she delivers sashes to the merchant.*
> *Strength and dignity are her clothing,*
> *and she laughs at the time to come.*
> *She opens her mouth with wisdom,*
> *and the teaching of kindness is on her tongue.*
> *She looks well to the ways of her household*
> *and does not eat the bread of idleness.*
> *Her children rise up and call her blessed;*
> *her husband also, and he praises her:*
> *"Many women have done excellently,*
> *but you surpass them all."*
> *Charm is deceitful, and beauty is vain,*
> *but a woman who fears the Lord is to be praised.*
> *Give her of the fruit of her hands,*
> *and let her works praise her in the gates. (Proverbs 31:10-31)*

This is the kind of woman you are looking for. This is who you need to pursue–charm is deceitful, beauty is vain–they will pass away. Pursue the Lord, Find a woman who is pursuing the Lord. Pursue that woman. Be bold, be a man of action!

Pursue other Men

It's time.

And Jesus went throughout all the cities and villages, teaching in their synagogues and proclaiming the gospel of the kingdom and healing every disease and every affliction. When he saw the crowds, he had compassion for them, because they were harassed and helpless, like sheep without a shepherd. Then he said to his disciples, "The harvest is plentiful, but the laborers are few; therefore pray earnestly to the Lord of the harvest to send out laborers into his harvest." (Matthew 9:35-38)

You are the laborers. If you have gone through Abide70 this far, you have to come to the realization that pointing outward, being on mission is the goal of what God has for us. Look around, who is in your sphere of influence? Who do you work with? Who are your unbelieving family members? Who do you workout with? Where do you like to recreate? Pursue. Pursue. Pursue these men, form a new group, go through Abide70 with them, point them to the truth. If you think you aren't ready, It is just an excuse, it is in the doing that you become ready.

Name Them!

Make a list of the different places where you have influence: write down the names of the men who you will begin pursuing: it may only be 1 or 2 at first, and there will be much failure and disappointment–do not become hardened: like our Lord, have compassion on the lost–pray for them! You have a high calling:

Therefore, we are ambassadors for Christ, God making his appeal through us. We implore you on behalf of Christ, be reconciled to God. (2 Corinthians 5:20)

Let us pursue, let us seek those who are lost, those who need to grow, and invite them to the feast!

Questions:

1. What does this look like right now—are you pursuing marriage? Are you in a relationship pursuing, do you want to be? What are your next steps in this? What are your expectations on how you will encourage your future wife in the Lord? How can we pray for you in this?

2. What is your role in leading kids in the body to Christ?

3. Do you feel equipped to lead your own Abide70 or a Bible study, or other curriculum) with a group of guys? What stops you from pursuing men like this?

4. Who are the guys you will be pursuing? What are you doing to pursue them, how can we pray for them by name?

Session 10:
Abide to the End

This is not the end. It's the beginning. If you are reading this, you have persevered through 10 weeks. You have spent hours in scripture that you might have not otherwise spent, you have some new habits and routines. Hopefully, you have a deeper love for Christ and a desire to serve others. Don't stop now—

On the last day of the feast, the great day, Jesus stood up and cried out, "If anyone thirsts, let him come to me and drink. Whoever believes in me, as the Scripture has said, 'Out of his heart will flow rivers of living water.'" (John 7:37-38)

Drink deeply and be filled with the Spirit of Christ—operate from the overflow! Don't turn back to scrolling and games and entertainment: there is something that is so much more satisfying—Christ and being on his mission This ends where it starts: the supremacy of Christ. He is King.

He is the image of the invisible God, the firstborn of all creation. For by him all things were created, in heaven and on earth, visible and invisible, whether thrones or dominions or rulers or authorities—all things were created through him and for him. And he is before all things, and in him all things hold together. (Colossians 1:15-17)

My hope is that as you have gone through the material, you have grown more and more aware of your need of the One who holds all things together, you have grown more and more aware of his grace and mercy, more aware of your sin, and more aware that any efforts that come from you are only done by his power, his working in you!

But God, being rich in mercy, because of the great love with which he loved us, even when we were dead in our trespasses, made us alive together with Christ—by grace you have been saved— and raised us up with him and seated us with him in the heavenly places in Christ Jesus, so that in the coming ages he might show the immeasurable riches of his grace in kindness toward us in Christ Jesus. For by grace you have been saved through faith. And this is not your own doing; it is the gift of God, not a result of works, so that no one may boast. For we are his workmanship, created in Christ Jesus for good works, which God prepared beforehand, that we should walk in them. (Ephesians 2:4-10, emphasis added)

Questions to Guide Your Life:

I have been asked the two following questions many times:

"If you knew you could not fail, what would you accomplish"
"What kind of man do you want to be?"
"What kind of man are you becoming right now?"

In our worldliness, we often jump to answers like "a successful business mogul, a professional athlete, a well-known pastor, a large charitable organizer" or some other dream—but let me cast in in a different light, starting with Scripture:

If you abide in me, and my words abide in you, ask whatever you wish, and it will be done for you. (John 15:7)

"Ask, and it will be given to you; seek, and you will find; knock, and it will be opened to you. (Matthew 7:7)

If we have the mind of Christ—if we are seeking the will of God, we cannot fail: God will not forsake us, God in his steadfast love remains ever faithful, and the end is sure:

After this I looked, and behold, a great multitude that no one could number, from every nation, from all tribes and peoples and languages, standing before the throne and before the Lamb, clothed in white robes, with palm branches in their hands, and crying out with a loud voice, "Salvation belongs to our God who sits on the throne, and to the Lamb!" And all the angels were standing around the throne and around the elders and the four living creatures, and they fell on their faces before the throne and worshiped God, saying, "Amen! Blessing and glory and wisdom and thanksgiving and honor and power and might be to our God forever and ever! Amen." (Revelation 7:9-12)

"Behold, I am coming soon, bringing my recompense with me, to repay each one for what he has done. I am the Alpha and the Omega, the first and the last, the beginning and the end." (Revelation 22:12-13)

He will wipe away every tear from their eyes, and death shall be no more, neither shall there be mourning, nor crying, nor pain anymore, for the former things have passed away. (Revelation 21:4)

For the Lamb in the midst of the throne will be their shepherd, and he will guide them to springs of living water, and God will wipe away every tear from their eyes." (Revelation 7:17)

If we truly believed this to be true, that this was our end, we know that we cannot fail—we would be men on mission for the sole end and glory of God. Now—we can—in obedience to the Lord, attempt anything—we cannot fail! If we are on mission, seeking the Glory of the Lord, we are no longer asking the question "How far can I go and not sin?" or "Is this thing sinful?" instead, we are looking at our lives and asking what is helpful for accomplishing the great mission of God? <u>What is hindering me?</u>

You cannot fail in being a man who leads your wife and kids in Christ—it is God who determines who comes to him.

You cannot fail in being a man who leads your co-workers to Jesus-it is God who determines who comes to him.

You cannot fail in being a man characterized by serving others-It is in Jesus Christ's power that you serve them!

You cannot fail even when you are the sinful man that you are (but don't use this as an excuse to sin—Romans 6:1!)-it is Christ who absorbs the sin and wrath of God's righteous anger—quickly turn back to Him!

From a worldly perspective we will experience successes and failures, but from an eternal perspective, men after Jesus' own heart can never fail because God's glorious purposes will be accomplished.

Persevere By God's Power

God through Jesus Christ sought us and created us so that we might enjoy him and give glory to him forever—let us press on—in assurance that he will hold us fast:

All that the Father gives Me will come to Me, and the one who comes to Me I will by no means cast out. (John 6:37 KJV)

My sheep hear my voice, and I know them, and they follow me. I give them eternal life, and they will never perish, and no one will snatch them out of my hand. My Father, who has given them to me, is greater than all, and no one is able to snatch them out of the Father's hand. I and the Father are one." (John 10:27-29)

And I am sure of this, that he who began a good work in you will bring it to completion at the day of Jesus Christ. (Philippians 1:6)

Who shall separate us from the love of Christ? Shall tribulation, or distress, or persecution, or famine, or nakedness, or danger, or sword? As it is written,

> *"For your sake we are being killed all the day long;*
>
> *we are regarded as sheep to be slaughtered."*

No, in all these things we are more than conquerors through him who loved us. For I am sure that neither death nor life, nor angels nor rulers, nor things present nor things to come, nor powers, nor height nor depth, nor anything else in all creation, will be able to separate us from the love of God in Christ Jesus our Lord. (Romans 8:35-39)

So let me encourage you once again brother!

Let us know; let us press on to know the Lord;
 his going out is sure as the dawn;
he will come to us as the showers,
 as the spring rains that water the earth." (Hosea 6:3)

Let us press on to know the God who loves us!

Reflect

Take some time and reflect on what you have learned–not necessarily from the lessons themselves, but in endeavoring to avail yourself of more time in the word, and in the Gospel-centered discussion with other men, in being in a vulnerable relationship with them.

Questions:

1. After this 10 weeks do you feel closer to the Lord? Do you feel closer to this group of men? Do you have a better feel for how you will continue to pursue God in the spiritual disciplines?

2. What lessons have you learned about yourself during this time? Do you feel like your newly developed habits will "stick"? What is your plan for sticking to your good habits? Will you go back to any of the habits that you had before?

3. What is next for you? Take some time to think about your ministry and review your mission: How does it flesh out, where will you plug in?

4. Do you want to have further conversations with someone in leadership to talk about what ministries you should be involved with? Do you have an idea of what is available in the body where you can formally and informally serve?

5. Develop a plan to maintain and strengthen guardrails and spiritual disciplines you intend to continue. Let other men in to know what these are. Memorialize your Mission statement and update it when your life changes–share it with men for accountability.

I pray that you continue to grow in the knowledge of our Lord Jesus Christ–that despite your failings, he would be your portion and your prize.

My flesh and my heart may fail,
　but God is the strength of my heart and my portion forever.
(Psalm 73:26)

The Lord is my chosen portion and my cup;
　you hold my lot.
 The lines have fallen for me in pleasant places;
　indeed, I have a beautiful inheritance.

You make known to me the path of life;
　in your presence there is fullness of joy;
　at your right hand are pleasures forevermore.
(Psalm 16:5-6,11),

the Lord bless you and keep you;
the Lord make his face to shine upon you and be gracious to you; the Lord lift up his countenance upon you and give you peace.
(Numbers 6:24-26)

Appendix of Resources:

Smartphone into Dumbphone Guide
What are the Spiritual Disciplines
Sample Mission Statement
I Need Help Now:

Smartphone into Dumbphone Guide:

Bottom line: you are addicted to your phone.

Cell phones and the apps that accompany are specifically created as a means to capture your attention, and in turn, your dollars. You may think that you can overcome the sophisticated algorithms invented to make sure you stay hooked, but this is a losing proposition, and deep down, you know it.

You nervously check your cell phone every few minutes (or seconds). At every ding, you look for your phone, seeing if you have a life-affirming "like" or text. You have anxiety when someone handles your phone or you think it is lost. Sometimes, you feel your phone buzz in your pocket–then realize your phone isn't even in your pocket. It is an idol.

So what do you do? Your life is at stake, though you don't believe it. If you continue on the path you are on, you WILL be owned by your device. You have to go to battle. This is about eye-gouging, hand-cutting violence for the sake of your purity and seeking of Christ.

In a different season, Billy Graham was known for calling ahead to the hotels he stayed in, and asking the hotel staff to remove the TV from his room. He knew that the price of a loss of purity, the shame connected to sin and the dishonoring of God wasn't worth even being close to the temptation. We carry something far more insidious in our pockets than a TV.

This guide is my attempt to share some of the best practices at dumbing down my phone to make it less attractive to me, to take it from being an idol. It is not meant to be extensive, or unbreakable, but it is meant to be a help.

Option 1: Get rid of your smartphone altogether and get a dumbphone. Something without the web, only with calling and maybe texting.

Since most people will recoil at that "I need 'x' app at work! I need it for 'x!'" I get it, just make sure your excuse isn't to protect your precious sin!

Option 2: Make your smartphone dumb. Here are some of the steps I have gone to in order to to this:

1. Get rid of the browser. Nothing good can come in through the browser that you can't wait and get later when you are sitting at a computer in a public place. Delete any other browsers.
Settings>Screen Time>Content and Privacy Restrictions>Allowed Apps>Safari

2. Get rid of email. Unless ONLY for work, email is a timewaster that can easily be accessed from a public computer.
Settings>Screen Time>Content and Privacy Restrictions>Allowed Apps>Mail

3. Get rid of game center. Dopamine is no good when it is for now purpose—only a timewaster.

Settings>Screen Time>Content and Privacy Restrictions>Allowed Apps>Game Center

4. Delete all apps that are time wasters, and they are almost all time wasters. Get extreme, and you can always add back in. I would recommend only having a good bible app, phone, text, maps alarm and any proprietary login app for work to start. I additionally have weather, music and podcasts and one banking app. podcasts can be a timewaster (can be browsed and used to download inappropriate podcasts, etc.) if you find that it wastes time—cut it off! Music ditto!

5. Get rid of the ability to download new apps. Settings>Screen Time> Content and Privacy Restrictions (on)>Itunes and App Store Purchases Settings>Screen Time>Content and Privacy Restrictions>Allowed Apps>App Store

6. Now the interesting part: once you have this very basic list, give your phone to a friend or spouse and have them change
     - Your itunes 4 digit passcode
     - Your itunes password

I know this can be circumvented, but this makes it difficult, and you have to engage in a conversation with your accountability partner or spouse if you want to download an app or especially if you 'cheat' and circumvent the system it cannot be 'locked' back to the state that you want it to be in without their help.

As a further "dumb" modification, you can change your screen to grayscale to make it less attractive.

Now turn off all notifications for apps you have left. Put the phone on silent as the default.

I have found this far more helpful than browser restrictions or monitoring apps. I have operated with a mostly dumb phone for years with minor inconvenience. It has been fine. Every once in a while it leads to a conversation as to why a would do such a thing—it often leads to a discussion about my own sin, confession and repentance, resulting in a boasting in Christ.

Remember why we do this: this isn't legalism (you cannot impose legalism on yourself!) and it isn't only about performance—this is about tilting the scales in your favor against a system that is severely, unfairly tilted against you. It is about freedom. We are commanded to do things in the Bible and especially prescient to cell phone use:

I will not set before my eyes
  anything that is worthless. (Psalm 101:3a)

Flee from sexual immorality. Every other sin a person commits is outside the body, but the sexually immoral person sins against his own body. (1 Corinthians 6:18)

Flee. Run with everything inside of you away from images and games that would distract you and weigh you down and run to Christ.

Therefore, since we are surrounded by so great a cloud of witnesses, let us also lay aside every weight, and sin which clings so closely, and let us run with endurance the race that is set before us, looking to Jesus, the founder and perfecter of our faith, who for the joy that was set before him endured the cross, despising the shame, and is seated at the right hand of the throne of God. (Hebrews 12:1-2)

Do what is commanded of you. Ask for the heart to do it for your joy in Christ.

Resource: The Spiritual Disciplines

We've all heard of the Spiritual disciplines, but what are they? Here is a great article by Donald Whitney, excerpted by Desiring God:

https://www.desiringgod.org/interviews/what-are-spiritual-disciplines

1. Personal and Corporate

First, the Bible prescribes both personal and interpersonal spiritual disciplines. There are those spiritual disciplines that we practice alone and those that we practice with other Christians. So, for example, we are to pray alone. That is a personal spiritual discipline. We are also to pray with the church. That is an interpersonal or congregational spiritual discipline.

We are to practice both because Jesus practiced both and because the Bible prescribes both of those for us. So we don't want to think of spirituality and the spiritual disciplines just as something we do by ourselves. We are to also engage others in the practice of the spiritual disciplines.

2. Doing and Being

A second characteristic of spiritual disciplines is that they are activities; they are not attitudes. Disciplines are practices. Spiritual disciplines are things you do. They are not character qualities. They are not graces. They are not the fruit of the Spirit. They are things you do.

So you read the Bible. That is something you do. That is a spiritual discipline. You meditate on Scripture. You pray, fast, worship, serve, learn, and so forth. These are activities. Now the goal of practicing any given discipline is not about doing as much as it is about being: being like Jesus, being with Jesus. But the biblical way to grow in being more like Jesus is through the rightly motivated doing of the biblical, spiritual disciplines.

The key verse in all this is 1 Timothy 4:7, which says, "Discipline yourself for the purpose of godliness" (NASB). The goal is godliness, but the biblical means to that is to discipline yourself by the power of the Holy Spirit, rightly motivated. We are to discipline ourselves for the purpose of godliness. The practical ways of doing that are things that you do.

Strictly speaking, joy is not a spiritual discipline. That is the fruit or the result of discipline done rightly. So it is that distinction between doing and being. And the spiritual disciplines are about doing. You can do them as a Pharisee. You can do them wrongly motivated. But rightly motivated, they are things that we are to do, in order to be like Jesus, to be with Jesus.

3. Modeled in the Bible

A third descriptor of the spiritual disciplines is that we are talking about things that are practices taught or modeled in the Bible. The reason that is important is otherwise we leave ourselves open to calling anything we want a spiritual discipline. So someone might say, "Gardening is a spiritual discipline for me," or "Exercise is one of my spiritual disciplines," or any other hobby or pleasurable habit they could call a spiritual discipline.

But one of the problems with that is that mindset could tempt someone to say, "Maybe meditation on Scripture works for you, but gardening does just as much for my soul as the Bible does for yours." Virtually anything being a spiritual discipline is one problem.

The other problem is that it leaves it to us to determine what will be best for our spiritual health and maturity rather than accepting those things God has revealed in Scripture as the means of experiencing God and growing in Christlikeness.

4. Promoted in the Scriptures

A fourth characteristic of spiritual disciplines is that those found in Scripture are sufficient for knowing and experiencing God and for growing in Christlikeness. We are told in the famous verses 2 Timothy 3:16–17 that "all Scripture is breathed out by God and profitable for teaching, for reproof, for correction, and for training in righteousness, that the man of God may be complete, equipped for every good work" — including the good work of pursuing the purpose of godliness, the good work of growing in Christlikeness. The Scriptures are sufficient for that.

So whatever else a person might claim regarding the spiritual benefits of some practice that is not in the Bible — something that maybe is promoted by some other spiritual cause or spiritual group or some spiritual leader, that if you will do this or you will do this or that, you will experience God, and it will be very meaningful — well, regardless of whatever benefit someone may claim accrues to them from that practice, at the very least we can say it isn't necessary. If it were necessary for spiritual maturity in godliness and progress in holiness, it would have been found and promoted in the Scriptures.

5. Derived from the Gospel

A fifth description of spiritual disciplines is that they are derived from the gospel, not divorced from the gospel. Rightly practiced, the spiritual disciplines take us deeper into the glories of the gospel of Jesus Christ, not away from it as though we have moved on to some advanced level of Christianity.

"The gospel is the ABCs. Now let's get into the really deep things of God: the spiritual disciplines." No, the spiritual disciplines are derived from the gospel, not divorced from it, and they only take us deeper into an understanding of the gospel.

6. Means, Not End

And the last characteristic of the spiritual disciplines is that they are means and not ends. The end — that is, the purpose of practicing the disciplines is godliness — is to "discipline yourself for the purpose of godliness" (1 Timothy 4:7 NASB).

And so we are not godly just because we practice the spiritual disciplines. That was the great error of the Pharisees. They felt by doing these things they were godly. No, they are not godliness in themselves, but rightly motivated, they are the means to godliness.

***

I want to emphasize that Abide70 is not designed to teach you how to pray or fast or read scripture. It is designed to put you in community and accountability with other brothers who are seeking to do these things as a regular pattern of their lives. There are fantastic resources for learning "the how" of Spiritual Disciplines. Don Whitney's books are a great start. If there is an area where you are weak—talk about it in the group and get strengthened and encouraged by brothers who are stronger in this area—iron sharpens iron!

Sample Mission Statement:

To joyfully proclaim the infinite glory of God and his son, Christ Jesus to:

- My wife
- My children
- My local gathering of believers, the Church.
- Non-believers (Work, Neighbors)

through exhortation, service and encouragement, empowered by the Holy Spirit, who lives in me.

My Mission is accomplished through:

1. Meeting with God, in prayer, word and worship daily, as my priority.
2. Simplifying my life and intake of entertainment and information, and limiting my reach relationally and proximally to be a good steward of time.
3. Regular, intentional family discipleship (1:1 and whole family)
4. Regular, intentional leading of my wife in prayer and date nights.
5. Regular, intentional, generous and spontaneous giving.
6. Serving others primarily in small group ministry.
7. Evangelism, primarily in the my neighborhood (specific families you are starting relationship with for the purpose of telling them the gospel and serving them) and through local men's workout group

(specific names), and with my co-workers (specific names)
8. Discipling men, specifically men in small group ministry (specific names) and developing discipleship materials for use by those who are discipling in the body.
9. Accountability this Mission and Vision will be given to and discussed with my wife and a few select brothers regularly. They are allowed to question and correct me in aligning my activities with this Mission.

Life Verse:

I have been crucified with Christ. It is no longer I who live, but Christ who lives in me. And the life I now live in the flesh I live by faith in the Son of God, who loved me and gave himself for me. (Galatians 2:20)

Word:
Joy, Consideration

My Mission will be hindered by my sins and inclinations/ my action against it

- Sullenness and Joylessness/ Seek my joy in Christ to play more, to be fun dad, fun husband, joyful dad, joyful husband, engaged friend.
- Materialism/ Practice simplicity, resist the pull of culture that more is better. Not browsing, Not shopping. Contentment in what Christ has provided abundantly for me.

- Approval Idols/ Prayer for my approval to only be found in the person of Christ—not clinging, but quietly suffering with Christ if I am actually being neglected.
- Lust/ By Holy Spirit power, fleeing from sexuality and sensuality, refusing to be "sucked in" by time wasting websites and images.
- Thought Life/ By Holy Spirit power, taking every thought captive and practicing imagining a far superior thought to any sinful thought, selfishness, feeling neglected, hurt, abused
- Stinginess/ Generosity to my Church, my Family, my Friends. Practicing openhandedness in all my possessions.
- Isolationism/ Being where others are and not hiding
- Grumbling, Putting others down/ Endeavor to speak well of others, and not put others down in order to feel good about myself.
- Selfishness/ Seek Christ's example of putting others first. Practice humility.

I Need Help <u>Now</u>:

Maybe you decided to go through the Abide70 curriculum as a means of growth and accountability, but now find yourself in a situation where you need more help:

- You have secret sin you need to repent of
- You have addiction that you feel you cannot get free of
- You are in a relationship that is destructive

Help comes from the Lord:

For we do not have a high priest who is unable to sympathize with our weaknesses, but one who in every respect has been tempted as we are, yet without sin. (Hebrews 4:15)

I lift up my eyes to the hills.
  From where does my help come?
My help comes from the Lord,
  who made heaven and earth.
He will not let your foot be moved;
  he who keeps you will not slumber.
Behold, he who keeps Israel
  will neither slumber nor sleep.
The Lord is your keeper;
  the Lord is your shade on your right hand.
The sun shall not strike you by day,
  nor the moon by night.
The Lord will keep you from all evil;
  he will keep your life.
The Lord will keep

*your going out and your coming in
from this time forth and forevermore. (Psalm 121)*

Come to me, all who labor and are heavy laden, and I will give you rest. (Matthew 11:28)

Don't rely on men—cry out to the Lord for deliverance. Pray for deliverance from sin and rest in the resurrection power of Christ! You "do" all the right things, but only God can give you a new heart and fill you with the Holy Spirit. God pours out wrath against sin, but he makes a way to be reconciled to his children.

*a bruised reed he will not break,
   and a faintly burning wick he will not quench;
   he will faithfully bring forth justice.
(Isaiah 42:3)*

Therefore he had to be made like his brothers in every respect, so that he might become a merciful and faithful high priest in the service of God, to make propitiation for the sins of the people. (Hebrews 2:17)

In this is love, not that we have loved God but that he loved us and sent his Son to be the propitiation for our sins. (1 John 4:10)

For if while we were enemies we were reconciled to God by the death of his Son, much more, now that we are reconciled, shall we be saved by his life. (Romans 5:10)

Help Comes From The Body:

Brothers, if anyone is caught in any transgression, you who are spiritual should restore him in a spirit of gentleness. Keep watch on yourself, lest you too be tempted. (Galatians 6:1)

You have brothers that are here to help. Talk to your Abide70 leader or small group leader or pastor and they will connect you to care.

Made in the USA
Monee, IL
03 October 2024